The
of Bl

Earl (

Also by Earl Ofari Hutchinson

The Myth of Black Capitalism
Let Your Motto Be Resistance
The Mugging of Black America
Black Fatherhood: The Guide to Male Parenting
Black Fatherhood II: Black Women Talk About Their Men
The Assassination of the Black Male Image
Beyond O.J.: Race, Sex, and Class Lessons for America
Blacks and Reds: Race and Class in Conflict, 1919-1990
Betrayed: Presidential Failure to Protect Black Lives
The Crisis in Black and Black

The Disapearance of Black Leadership

Earl Ofari Hutchinson, Ph.D.

Middle Passage Press, Inc.
Los Angeles, CA

Middle Passage Press, Inc.
5517 Secrest Drive
Los Angeles, CA 90043

**Publisher's Cataloging-in-Publication
(Provided by Quality Books, Inc.)**

Hutchinson, Earl Ofari.
　　The disappearance of Black leadership / by Earl Ofari Hutchinson. — 1st ed.
　　　p. cm.
　　Includes bibliographical references and index.
　　LCCN : 99-80025
　　ISBN : 1-881032-16-7

　　1. Afro-American leadership. 2. Afro-American politicians. 3. Afro-Americans — Politics and government. 4. Racism. 5. Racism in mass media. 6. Afro-Americans — Economic conditions. 7. Afro-Americans — Social conditions.　I. Title.

E185.615.H88 2000　　　　303.3/4/08996073
　　　　　　　　　　　　　　QBI99-500567

Acknowledgements

I am truly blessed and thankful to have a caring, committed circle of friends. They have given me invaluable suggestions, comments, and criticisms. I have learned to listen closely to their words. They possess great wisdom and insight. They are always on point thanks again for everything Barbara Bramwell, Rene Childress, and Matt Blair.

Dedication

To those who showed us the way, and to those who will show us the way again.

Contents

Introduction: Where Are the Black Leaders?   1
I   The Shameful Silence of Too Many Black Ministers   13
II   The Dilemma of Two Kings   29
III   Whither the Congressional Black Caucus?   39
IV   The Tattered Tale of Two Icons   51
V   Why Speak for Black Women   61
VI   Black Politicians: Lost, Stolen, and Strayed   73
VII   Remembering the *Real* Black Panther Party   83
VIII The Jesse Factor   91
IX   Who Is Listening To Us?   105
X   Another Image for the NAACP   115
XI   The Unselling of Malcolm X   127
XII   The Elixir of Wealth   133
Conclusion: The Reappearance of Black Leadership   147
Postscript: Blueprint for Seizing Leadership   155
Bibliography   163
Reference Notes   166
Index   180

Introduction
Where Are the Black Leaders?

I ARRIVED AT THE PRESS conference held in July 1998 at a local community center in Los Angeles with much hope. The press conference was called by a local black activist to express outrage over the rape and murder of Sherrice Iverson, a 7-year-old African-American girl, in the women's restroom at a Nevada casino in May 1997. Jeremy Strohmeyer, a white teenager from a prosperous, suburban home, was charged with the murder. The slaying was horrid enough. But what was even more sickening was that Strohmeyer's friend, David Cash, who witnessed at least part of the gruesome assault on Iverson, did nothing to stop it and did not tell authorities about the murder afterwards. This sparked mass public disgust and anger.

There were two reasons why I was hopeful about the press conference. I thought that it was a brutally compelling story that black activists and community leaders in Los Angeles and nationally could use to draw public attention to the cataclysmic problems of sexual victimization, racially-motivated violence aimed particularly at poor blacks and children, the disparities in the criminal justice system in reference to the punishment of whites versus blacks, and public indifference to violence against African-Americans, especially, African-American women. I had planned to devote one of my weekly syndicated newspaper columns to the Iverson case. I wanted to focus as much public attention as possible on these issues. It was not simply black adults being murdered, now it was a black child.

I was hopeful about the press conference for another reason. I expected leaders from such organizations as the NAACP, Congress of Racial Equality (CORE), Southern Christian Leadership Conference (SCLC), the Urban League, and the Nation of Islam to stumble over each other to use the Iverson case as their bully pulpit to shame, coax, and prod the public and elected officials to take immediate action on child protective legislation, greater funding for child services, more aid to victims of violence, and, of course, the full prosecution of Strohmeyer and Cash. I was wrong. Not one person from these organizations showed up at the press conference to voice any of these demands or to express their personal concern about the killing or to give support to the Iverson family.

At the close of the press conference, I cornered one of the Iverson family supporters and casually asked: "Where are the black leaders?" I thought perhaps they were not there because they were not invited to participate. He shrugged, sighed, and raised his hands upward in resignation. He indicated that

Iverson was murdered nearly a year ago and that not one of the established black leaders had spoken out about the racial and sexual implications of the murder during that time. Therefore he felt it was a waste of time to approach them. The fact that he felt this way about them was a tragedy almost as great as the murder of Iverson.

The Iverson case was a volatile and heartbreaking case. It was pregnant with the gripping social issues that sledgehammer blacks. The leaders should have been there whether formally invited or not. I knew that many of them were often outspoken on issues such as police abuse, housing and job discrimination, education, health care, and media racism.

I wondered whether his profound disgust with mainstream black leaders was due to the fact that many of them are mostly middle-class business and professional persons. The Iverson case involved the often murky issue of crime and violence aimed at poor and working class blacks.

This issue often makes many traditional black leaders squeamish. They view issues such as these with a strange blend of caution, uncertainty, and wariness. Or was his feeling of disgust with them due to the fact that Iverson did not carry their official imprimatur as an issue the leaders could neatly package, design a protest campaign around their own demands, and maintain control of? Or was his feeling of disgust due to the fact that leadership in the 1990s had been turned into a corporate style competitive business where established organizations often pick and choose low risk, high profile glitter issues to enhance their prestige and authority? These are the kind of issues that can be comfortably converted into dollars and patronage from politicians, government agencies, and corporate officials.

Or was his feeling of disgust with the mainstream black leaders due to the old tail wagging the dog syndrome where black communities spontaneously react with rage to an appalling atrocity and catch black leaders napping? They are then forced to scramble to catch up and reassert their leadership.

His feeling of disgust with these leaders was probably due to all of these reasons. Still, I believed that when the extreme gravity of the issues in the Iverson tragedy became more apparent a few leaders would quickly take up the cause. Over the next few weeks the Iverson case drew huge amounts of favorable national press coverage. Iverson family members appeared on major talk shows. There was an avalanche of letters and calls that poured in from outraged persons, including many whites and non-blacks who expressed great sympathy for the victim, and offered to help in the drive for the prosecution of Cash and the harshest possible sentence for Strohmeyer. Congressional leaders and legislators in several states rushed bills through to strengthen child protective laws.

But even after Nevada prosecutors in the Iverson case made it clear that they believed Iverson's murder was in part racially motivated, the silence from local and national black leaders such as the NAACP, CORE, SCLC, the Urban League, and the Nation of Islam as well as black elected officials was still just as deafening.

●●●●●●

In part from frustration, and in part from genuine puzzlement, I asked myself: What happened to the Malcolm Xs, the Martin Luther Kings, the Roy Wilkins, Elijah Muhammads, Stokeley Carmichaels, Huey Newtons, Rosa Parks, Thurgood Marshalls, Whitney Youngs, A. Phillip Randolphs, and Fannie Lou Hamers. The outspoken leaders of years gone by. Why is it after nearly two generations have passed by no leader of their stature has emerged to give voice to the frustrations of the black middle-class and needs of the black poor?

My goal in *The Disappearance of Black Leadership* is to find an answer to that question. In this book, I looked closely at the traditional black organizations and leadership that directly grew out of, or were deeply influenced by, the old civil rights movement. These leaders claim to speak for most black Americans. This is why I ask, where are the leaders today like those who throughout the history of the black struggle in America continually stormed the barricades for social change? Where are the leaders whose stirring words inspired blacks to march, picket, and protest against racism and injustice?

Where are the leaders whose passionate appeals for justice commanded the attention and the respect of the nation and the world? These leaders made their organizations—the NAACP, Black Panthers, SCLC, SNCC, Urban League, and the Nation of Islam—household names among many blacks.

Despite the fierce ideological differences that raged between them, blacks knew that these organizations would be militant, uncompromising advocates for the black dispossessed, and relentlessly battle for economic and political empowerment, civil rights, and social justice. Their diverse programs and tactics offered something for everyone—black nationalism or integration, social equality or social separation, black capitalism or black socialism. When a crisis arose, and there always was one, blacks could depend on these organizations and leaders to operate like a quick response team and launch an instant strike with a protest march, demonstration, boycott, or lawsuit.

Some say that it is naive, and unrealistic to expect anything like that to happen today. After all, the 1960s were a time of ferment and rising consciousness by people of color. Black leaders and their organizations often heroically reflected the challenge and spirit of those times. Those times, they say, exist only in the minds of a few disgruntled activists who nostalgically long for a romanticized past that exists only in history books, memoirs of former civil rights leaders, or their imaginations.

The 1990s and the march into the next millennium, they claim, marked the death of social ferment. It was slain by the reality that more blacks than ever have come closer to realizing the American Dream. They own more homes and businesses. They have shattered the glass in the glass ceiling in corporations and the professions. They hold more elected offices and spots in government. They are healthier and better educated. They have politically and economically bloomed like never before in the history of America. Their leaders and organizations have shifted with the times and now rightly focus on grabbing even more of that wealth and political power.

This success theme is not total fiction. It is the reality for many blacks. But this tale of nirvana only tells part of the story, and even in that part it is jam-packed with many delusions. It glosses over the reality that blacks are two and three times more likely to be unemployed than whites, trapped in segregated neighborhoods, and their kids attend segregated schools.

It ignores the reality that young black males and females are far more likely to be murdered, suffer HIV/AIDS affliction, to be harassed "Driving While Black," racially-profiled, jailed, on probation or parole, permanently barred in many states from voting because of felony convictions, and more likely to be victims of racially motivated violence than whites. It downplays the reality that black children are more likely to be neglected, mistreated by social service agencies, and homeless. It blurs the reality that blacks, rich and poor, are still viciously savaged by much of the media and the public as menaces to society and ridiculed as clowns, coons, and mammies on goof ball sit-coms, or ethnically cleansed from network TV.

Many middle-class blacks find the new suburban neighborhoods they moved to are resegregated and soon look like the old neighborhoods they fled. They are ignored by cab drivers, followed by clerks in stores, left fuming at restaurants because of poor or no service, find that more and more of their sons and daughters are cut out of scholarships and student support programs at universities because of the demolition of affirmative action, and denied bank and thrift agency loans for their businesses and homes.

Then there is the much vaunted fantasy that the gates of

corporate America have swung completely off their hinges for blacks. Many major companies issue flowery press releases, brochures, assorted handouts and annual stockholder reports boasting of their commitment to diversity. They appear on the surface to be in full compliance with federal equal opportunity guidelines, have well-established programs for hiring, training, and the promotion of minorites, have more black faces in visible corporate management positions and a few name blacks that sit on corporate boards of directors.

But there is a sinister side that tells a story less of equal opportunity and more of corporate apartheid. In 1999, black CEOs at the Fortune 1000 corporations were still relative rarities. Nearly ten out of ten senior managers were white males and black managers are paid on average less than their white counterparts. Even inside the corridors of corporate America, many black executives find themselves stuck in the same dead end positions while younger, white men and women zoom by them up the fast track ladder.

Many more find they are stacked into the corporate ghetto jobs or positions such as director, VP, or manager of community relations, equal opportunity, or human resources departments. They are assigned to oversee "special markets" (i.e. black and minority) and are ostracized at, or excluded from, company social functions.

They have filed law suits, threatened boycotts, pushed selective buying campaigns, staged demonstrations, and mounted letter writing campaigns against dozens of corporations to try to get them to clean up their discriminatory act.

However corporate apartheid still storms through the plush corridors and suites of many companies.

••••••

The grimmer part of all this is that the get rich quick days of the Clinton years in the 1990s were fragile and tenuous at best for many blacks. Clinton could never be confused with a liberal Democrat no matter how hard Republicans tried to sell the idea that he was. His tepid political centrism did include a slight nod to black interests. This was just enough to hold in check some of the worst atrocities plotted by Republican Gothics such as one-time congressman Newt Gingrich, Mississippi Senator Trent Lott, nearly all the Supreme Court justices, and many state legislators and governors.

If they had their total way they would have happily taken back every one of the political and social gains blacks, other minorities, and women have made since the 1960s and turned America into something more akin to a police state in progress than a democracy. The rush towards an even more conservative America in the new millennium holds great peril for blacks. The likelihood is that more Americans than ever will retreat to the know-nothingism ushered in during the Reagan years of the 1980s and refined during the Clinton years in the 1990s.

There is the potentially even more lethal prospect that a kinder, gentler, sneakier political conservatism will annihilate the residue of civil rights, civil liberties, social, and education programs still on the books. This would totally remake America's political landscape in the early years of the new Millennium.

Despite the notion that the 1960s is and should be long dead and buried, the next Millennium will be every bit a time of crisis and challenge as were the 1960s. This is not a doomsday scenario. It is a wake-up call for more cutting edge social activist leaders like the ones who brought America the great social, political, and economic gains of the 1960s.

Some will argue that there is a national leader and groups who already fit that bill. The leader, they say, is Nation of Islam head Louis Farrakhan. He has commanded the fear and respect of whites, many middle-class blacks, and poor and working class blacks. He has a message, an organization, a program, and a national and international following. He pulled off one of the greatest organizational coups in living memory during the 1990s with the Million Man March in 1995.

There is also the Black Radical Congress, an eclectic collection of students, professors, community activists, labor and womens group members, and a smattering of unreconstructed 1960 black militants. The group met in Chicago in 1998 and pieced together a social action program that on paper at least dealt with the needs of poor and working class blacks.

I do not deal with either Farrakhan or the Congress in this book. I have written extensively on Farrakhan in my two previous books. *The Crisis in Black and Black* and *The Assassination of the Black Male Image*. I have spent considerable time detailing the prospects and problems with his leadership. As for the Congress, their organizers must be commended for their willingness to champion the cause of the black poor. But the group is much too new, and the jury is way out on what, or even whether, it can provide an effective model for leadership and community organizing over the long haul. So far, other than its initial gathering, a handful of position papers, a Internet chat site, and setting up a handful of local chapters, the Black Radical Congress has not registered a blip on the radar chart in black communities.

This is why I ask, where are the leaders who are prepared to shoulder the same burdens and rise to the same heights of leadership of past years. In asking this question there is a massive caveat. Leaders are not sustained by the cult of personality or the aura of an individual. Leaders are not those who have a knack for sound bites and photo-ops. Leaders are not celebrities, entertainers, movie stars, or athletes simply because they are highly paid, highly written about, and highly visible. Leaders are not appointed, anointed, designated, declared, or propped up by the media or the corporate or political structure. Leaders are not those who substitute phrase mongering for a workable agenda and a constituency.

Many blacks have accepted or mistaken these types as leaders for a simple reason. Blacks have been tossed to the far flung margins of American society and are desperate to find someone, anyone, who appears to speak boldly on their behalf. The susceptibility of many blacks to embrace this type of leader has been the cause of such profound pessimism about what and who a leader is and should be that many blacks have thrown up their hands in disgust. They brand black leaders, in some cases all black leaders, as corrupt, ineffective, selfish, and weak; and loudly declare that blacks should wish pox on anybody or any group that is called or call themselves leaders.

Despite the legitimate bitterness and disappointment many blacks feel about black leaders, there are many men and women with energy, commitment, have a program, possess an outrage over conditions, a vision of change, and are willing to take action. They are leaders and in the new Millennium they will be badly needed.

While I tell in this book why many black leaders have disappeared, I also tell how the men and women who fit the true bill of leaders can and must reappear.

I
The Shameful Silence
of Too Many Black Ministers

I WAS AMONG THE SMALL knot of people that had gathered on the busy mid-town Los Angeles street corner. This was the corner where Margaret Laverne Mitchell, a 54-year-old, homeless, mentally disturbed, African-American woman, was gunned down by a Los Angeles police officer on May 21, 1999. Mitchell was stopped for questioning about an alleged pilfered shopping cart from a local supermarket. Police claimed that they shot her when she lunged at them with a screwdriver. However, several eyewitnesses said that she did not pose a threat to the officers and was shot as she walked away.

This was only one shooting in a string of several outrageous and spectacular shootings of mostly unarmed African-Americans by the police. This seemed part of the deadly pattern of Wild West style, shoot-first-and-ask-questions-later violence by police when the alleged culprits are black. The shooting rocked the city and kindled protests, demonstrations, rallies, and demands for federal probes of police abuse.

This particular day the small group had gathered to pay tribute to Mitchell. We were led in prayer by a Latino Catholic priest. In the coming days Jewish and Catholic worshippers would also offer prayers for Mitchell.

During the next month many persons of varied religious persuasions felt compelled to pay religious homage to Mitchell. Many persons that is except black ministers. In the month after Mitchell was shot there was no public record that any one of the dozens of black ministers in Los Angeles expressed any public outrage over the shooting. There was also no sign that any black church leader had taken a moment to stop on the corner and say a simple prayer of remembrance for Mitchell.

This shameful silence by black ministers on the Mitchell slaying was especially galling considering that her tragic death dramatically focused public attention on the issues of poverty, homelessness, race and gender discrimination, the shabby treatment of needy persons who suffer mental disorders, and police abuse. One would have thought that these crucial issues would have evoked an instant public outcry from black ministers. But this time they did not.

• • • • • •

Dr. Martin Luther King, Jr. was also deeply troubled by the silence of many black ministers on social justice issues. He repeatedly blasted those black ministers who were eternally locked into a hunt for higher offices, fund raising drives, building campaigns, revivals, testimonial dinners, and pastor appreciation days.

Their abysmal failure to take leadership in the struggle for civil rights and social justice, he felt, was disgraceful and damaging to African-Americans. King also lashed out hard at them because he knew three crucial things about the black church.

He knew that the black church was borne in oppression and baptized in struggle. From the moment that Richard Allen, Absalom Jones, and another member were dragged from their knees while praying in a white section of the St. George Methodist Episcopal Church in Philadelphia in 1786, and then formed the Free African Society, black churches and their ministers have waged a feverish fight against slavery and racial discrimination.

Their churches organized mutual aid societies for the economic care and uplift of blacks, provided meeting places for abolitionists, gave sanctuary to fugitive slaves, and offered protection against racist attacks. Nearly every black minister of the pre-Civil War era blazed their name on the heroic page of the great struggle to abolish slavery. And that is why they are worth remembering today.

King also knew that in many churches the black minister is the supreme potentate and autocrat whose word is law. He continually reminds his flock and his church's hierarchy that he is "anointed" or even "appointed" by God to deliver the word. This automatically exempts him from any question or challenge to his authority. To do this would be to risk being denounced for blasphemy since challenging the minister was tantamount to challenging God.

Many ministers solidified their exalted standing by cultivating the ability to perform verbal gymnastics, refining their showman techniques to better dazzle and mesmerize crowds, and by steeping themselves in esoteric biblical lore. Some never missed the chance to audaciously manipulate the emotions of their flock. One word from the minister could galvanize large numbers of persons to do just about anything that he deemed worthwhile in the name of God.

Many black ministers also recognized that as long as they confined their message to a fundamentalist interpretation of biblical scripture they posed no threat to white authority and were generally left alone. As a bonus for strictly confining their message to an otherworldly promise of deliverance from evil, they even got occasional favors from politicians and business leaders.

This appearance of independence or being connected further enhanced their authority, dominance, and stature in the eyes of many in their flock. This was an enormous concentration of power in the pulpit that could be used for good or bad, and everything in between.

King further knew that despite the towering disenchantment, criticism, and desertions of many church faithful, the black church commanded the steel-clad respect and allegiance of millions of African-Americans who willingly poured their time, money and energy into church functions.

••••••

There were many moments during the 20th Century when many black church ministers awoke from their slumber and threw their weight behind the civil rights and political empowerment movements.

The most notable minister to storm to the forefront on social issues was Adam Clayton Powell, Sr., in the 1920s, and his even better known son, Adam Clayton Powell Jr., in the 1930s and 1940s. They were pastors of Harlem's Abyssinian Baptist Church, the nation's largest black church. The elder Powell combined in his church the perfect blend of charitable service and social activism by establishing dozens of ministries to feed and clothe the poor, minister to and provide shelter for the sick, and develop and support black businesses.

Powell Jr. railed against those black preachers he labeled "theological twisters," "ministerial mountebanks," "pulpit pounders," and "clerical clowns." He demanded that ministers shape up and become "men who will teach and lead the masses into a just way of life." With the elder Powell's full approval, Powell Jr. more than practiced what he preached. During the depths of the 1930s Great Depression and the early years of World War II; he formed the Peoples Committee, the United Negro Bus Strike Committee, the Greater New York Coordinating Committee, and the Citizens Committee on the Conditions at Harlem Hospital. They held tumultuous demonstrations, rallies, picket lines, and boycotts to fight for more and better jobs, quality health care, for increased political representation, and against discrimination.

The Powells were hardly alone in championing social activism among ministers in the immediate pre-World War II years. During the 1930s, a number of the NAACP chapters were organized and led by black ministers. When no one else would dare open their doors to the NAACP members for meetings, many black churches did.

Those ministers energized the black masses, rocked the politicians back on their heels, and reshaped the social and economic tapestry for blacks in many Northern cities. They established a model and standard of social activist leadership within the black church that would not be duplicated on this large a scale again until Martin Luther King and his core of minister leaders-followers came along a generation later to escalate the 1960s civil rights movement.

•••••

The escalation of civil rights activities and involvement snapped many black ministers to attention. Even then, despite what many believed in the 1990s, the black church was not the only or even the major player in civil rights battles. Many ministers refused to budge an inch to help civil rights protesters. They remained rooted deep in biblical dogma, fear, and accommodation. In many cities business leaders, teachers, labor unions, womens groups, and students were far more active than ministers in sparking and spearheading marches, demonstrations, rallies, boycotts, and political lobbying for civil rights. Ministers such as King who were the most active in the civil rights movement beginning in the late 1950s were generally part of secular organizations that operated far outside the church orbit. It was the glacial silence of many ministers that most irritated those ministers who did take strong stands against racism and poverty.

In 1966, the National Committee of Black Churchmen which included some of the nation's leading black church leaders took out a full-page ad in the *New York Times*. They sharply criticized black ministers for their "distorted" and "complacent" emphasis on chariot over Jordan sermons while turning a blind eye toward the civil rights and black power battles.

Those church leaders pledged to devote their resources and energies to that battle. Some black ministers heeded their call but many others still resisted it. Their fierce fights against the progressive black ministers wracked several denominations.

In 1961, King found out how powerful the hostility and fear of many black ministers was toward any kind of involvement in the civil rights movement. At the National Baptist Convention, the largest black religious group in America, King and a band of dissidents challenged the ultra-conservative leaders of the group to give more active support to the civil rights battles. The Convention was dominated by the tyrannical, autocratic, hyper-paranoid Joseph. H. Jackson. This was the same organization that King had been weaned on practically from the cradle. His father Martin Luther King, Sr. or "Daddy King" had been life long pals with all the key players in the group, and that included Jackson.

Friendship and blood ties did not matter when the showdown came. Jackson and his hard core fundamentalist men of the cloth twisted, cajoled, promised favors, and tossed money to keep their men in line. They flung unchristian-like threats and insults at the civil rights advocate-ministers, engaged in fisti-cuffs with them, and slandered King as a "hoodlum and crook."

When the dust settled, King's slate of progressive ministers was soundly thrashed and he found himself summarily booted out of the organization. Jackson was not finished with King and the civil rights supporters. He banned his cronies from attend-ing civil rights conferences or events, and anything else that had even the remotest taint of civil rights. Jackson left no doubt where he stood when the Convention in 1980 endorsed Ronald Reagan for president. Just to show this was not the xenophobic political reaction of an aging, cantankerous, reactionary, reli-gious demagogue, his successor T.J. Jemison happily endorsed Reagan again in 1984.

And finally, in the climax of personal pique Jackson spent more than $50,000 to brick up the doors on the side of his Chicago church when the street it faced was renamed Martin Luther King Jr. Drive.

●●●●●●●

Despite King's warnings and admonitions about complacency in the black church, and the villainous treatment he received at the hands of many of his minister brethren in the 1950s his worst fears came true in the 1990s. Many black ministers and church members were stone silent on the rollback of affirmative action, the assault on civil liberties, the gutting of job and social programs, the slash in health care programs, the disparity in the criminal justice system, the rise in racially-motivated violence, the deterioration in public education, the draconian cuts in welfare, the surge in police abuse, and homelessness during the 1980s and 1990s.

There are several bad reasons why those conditions have become social plagues. Start with the money grab. The phrase greed is not enough was an apt one for the 1990s. Hyper-greed polluted much of America from Wall Street to back street USA. The money grab seeped into the pulpits of many black churches and chased out the old values of human caring, sharing, empathy, and compassion.

Those ministers who succumbed to the temptations of greed began casting a deft eye at other ministers and saw them less and less as brethren and men and women of the cloth, whose sole concern should be the business of saving souls. Rather they now saw them more and more as dog-eat-dog competitors whose sole concern was the business of hoarding the most dollars. They measured their success by the height and glitter of new buildings and the heaps of expensive furnishings they could pack in them. The game now was to see who could be the minister that stood at the top of the religious deck.

The ministers who played the game the best were able to curry the good graces of mayors, city councilpersons, alderpersons, state and federal officials, corporate leaders and bank lenders. This was seen by them as a minimum prerequisite to get business and construction grants and loans, building permits and zoning variances for their plush new edifices. The game also required that they not say or do anything that was viewed by the political and business establishment as threatening their authority.

In other words, many of these ministers were solely after money and political favors. They could hardly be expected to turn around after getting their rewards and advocate demonstrations and protests against those same mayors, city officials, corporations and banks for job and housing discrimination, redlining, police abuse, or for not providing adequate municipal services in the poorest black communities.

• • • • • •

There are three especially burning issues in which the silence by many black ministers has left many African-Americans politically confused, socially stunted, and physically at risk.

• **Police Violence.** In his radio address in April 1999, President Bill Clinton said that he was "deeply disturbed" about police violence. And well he should have been. The shootings of Amadou Diallo in New York in February 1999, and Tyisha Miller in Riverside, California in December 1998 by white police officers were high profile cases that brought thousands of protesters into the streets. Yet they were only the gruesome tip of the ice berg. The number of police abuse complaints had steadily climbed throughout the 1990s. The nearly 12,000 complaints nationally of police abuse in 1996 almost matched the total number for the entire period from 1984 to 1990.

With the notable exceptions of the Reverends Al Sharpton

and Herbert Daughtry in New York, the Reverend Paul Jakes in Chicago, and a meager handful of local ministers in other cities, in groups such as the National Progressive Baptist Convention, the invisibility of black ministers on the issue of police abuse was just as glaring in other cities. There were many members in the congregations of every black church who had suffered abuse or harassment; or had friends, relatives, or acquaintances who had. There were thousands of young black males and females who attended these churches who were at the severest of risk from police harassment or violence.

In many congregations there were also judges, prosecutors, police officials, and officers. A word or two from the pulpit by the minister would have prompted discussions among them about the need for fairness and justice in law enforcement, and the search for ways to keep their members as far as possible out of harm's path.

• **The HIV/AIDS Crisis.** By the mid-1990s, African-Americans accounted for more than forty percent of AIDS cases in the United States. By the close of the year 2000, if the rampaging upward trend in the disease among blacks is not checked, the estimate was that blacks would make-up half of all AIDS cases in the country. As the HIV/AIDS death toll soared among African-Americans, many black church leaders ignored it, vehemently denied that it was a major problem, or simply declared it a "white gay disease." They flipped to the oft-cited line in *Leviticus* in the Bible that condemned homosexuality as "an abomination" and self-righteously dismissed those who contracted the disease as sinful and shameful, and branded them as threats to the stability of the black family.

When pro football star Reggie White caught heavy flak in 1997 for his silly, vain, and disgusting verbal mugging of gays he quickly ducked behind biblical lore to justify his remarks. The gospel singing Winans sisters drew equally heavy fire from gay groups the same year for their anti-gay single, "Not Natural." Yet there were no major protests within black churches against their repulsive lyrics and the sales of their records leaped. All of them, it seemed, had developed an intense case of collective amnesia to other passages in the bible that command and demand tolerance and respect for differences among people, and that includes different personal lifestyles too. And many ministers said not a mumbling word to their flock that political disfranchisement, poverty, double-digit unemployment, imprisonment, and chronic disease were the real ills that sliced up black families.

It took a rash of government reports, TV specials, and newspaper stories about the soaring body count from AIDS, and the growing awareness and alarm by many African-Americans about the catastrophe of AIDS in 1998 and 1999 before some black church leaders tepidly broke their conspiracy of silence. They scrambled to sponsor AIDS speak outs and AIDS Awareness days.

Even with the lure of state and federal grants for AIDS education, many hedged their bets by paying lip service to the AIDS crisis but doing little to provide educational materials, counseling, and agency referral to members or the AIDS afflicted. Fewer still actively encourage their followers to get involved with groups that campaign and lobby for greater funding and more programs for AIDS education and treatment.

•**Personal Corruption.** In February 1999, a Florida jury convicted

Dr. Henry Lyons, president of the National Baptist Convention USA, the country's biggest and most influential black religious organization of racketeering and grand theft. He pled guilty to tax fraud in federal court. He was sentenced to 5-1/2 years in state prison, 4 years in federal prison, and ordered to pay millions in restitution. There was a galaxy of evidence that Lyons stole the money, cavorted with his mistress, flaunted his opulent lifestyle, and thumbed his nose at other church leaders and those in his own flock who questioned his moral decadence.

Yet many black ministers, before and during his trial, and after his conviction, stood shoulder to shoulder with him in press conferences and interviews, patted him on the back in support. They took up his self-serving wail that he was being persecuted as part of a white racist conspiracy.

After Lyons apologized to the court for playing the race card and admitted his guilt, many of the ministers did not recant their support. Their silence was an open signal that they believed that prominent ministers who lie, cheat, play fast and loose with the hard earned dollars of their flock, and then try to weasel out of punishment for their misconduct are still worthy of pity, even praise.

Most black ministers it appears do not engage in the blatant thievery Lyons did and put in long hours ministering to their members, developing their ministries, and expanding their outreach programs. But many others are blissfully mired in a single-minded pursuit to build showy and pricey new buildings, purchase glittering furnishings, haul in inflated salaries, pad expense accounts, take globe-trotting trips, and make endless pitches for collections. Their brandishing of fancy cars, expensive homes, clothes, and jewelry has done much to fan the popular public image of black ministers as charlatans or "pimps in the pulpit" as some blacks even more irreverently brand them.

••••••

There are as many Christian denominations, sects, and cults as there are types of ministers, styles, and scriptural interpretations under the sun within black communities. When stripped away, however, there are three distinct types of ministers and churches.

The first type of minister Martin Luther King, Jr. and the Adam Clayton Powell, Sr. and Jr. would vigorously applaud. They diligently follow the biblical admonition in *Luke*, "He has scattered the proud . . . and the rich he has sent empty away." These ministers unhesitantly preach a message of redemption and salvation through peace, justice, and social activism.

They joyfully open their meeting halls and sanctuaries to community organizations to hold meetings, rallies, plan marches and demonstrations, circulate petitions, write letters, faxes, and emails on such issues as police abuse, job and housing discrimination, redlining, poor public schools, and neighborhood services. They hold forums, discussions, workshops, educational sessions, and sponsor community events on social and political issues. They have intensely proactive ministries to help and counsel the homeless, HIV/ AIDS afflicted, prisoners, battered women, at risk young men and women, and local entrepreneurs. They can always be found on the front-line of social action.

The second type of minister King and the Powells would be less happy with. However, they would still praise their work as far as it goes. These ministers diligently follow the admonition in *Numbers*, "And your children shall be shepherds in the wilderness . . . and shall suffer for your faithlessness." They blend the traditional doctrinal message of redemption through moral cleansing with an occasional bit of social activism such as hosting voter registration campaigns, business conferences, job and skills training, and corporate job recruiting fairs. They have limited ministries that counsel the homeless, prisoners, and at risk youth. Occasionally they can be found on the front-line of social action.

The third type of minister King and the Powell, Sr. and Jr. spent a considerable amount of their time and energy railing against. They are perfectly content to follow the admonition, "Seek first the kingdom of God and its righteousness and all these other things will be added unto you." They absolutely reject the notion that the path to redemption and salvation is through involvement in social causes.

They stage plays, musicals, hold endless bible study courses, revivals, prayer sessions, deliver tough line fundamentalist fire and brimstone damnation in—hell, and salvation-in-the-sky sermons. Whatever temporal message they have is aimed at denouncing gays, alcohol, drugs, and sexual profligacy. They have almost no active ministries and limit their skimpy aid and assistance to their own members. They tolerate no criticism of their word or deeds.

Many ministers are scrupulously honest, devout, and truly belief that it is dangerous heresy to mix politics with religion. Others such as Lyons use religious fundamentalism to mask their own personal corruption and decadence. Many more use it as a cover to duck social issues. They believe that to take stands on social and political issues is risky business and would severely jeopardize their chance of winning favors, patronage, donations, and securing loans, and other funds from politicians and business leaders.

Many black ministers make a mighty effort to address deep seated social ills and use their influence to be spiritual mentors and social advocates. But far too many do not. The black ministers that slump into complacency and social stagnation, and who are hopelessly enmeshed in greed and personal aggrandizement have rejected Dr. King's call to take the front line in the battle for social justice. They forget or ignore the entreaty in *Luke* to "put down the mighty from their thrones, and exalt those of low degree." The failure of many black ministers to provide the strong direction and leadership to combat the devastating social and economic crisis problems that have piled up on the doorsteps of many blacks, especially the black poor, during the 1990s has helped to spirtually and socially disarm many African-Americans. This is the byproduct of the shameful silence of too many black ministers.

II
The Dilemma of Two Kings

I LISTENED WITH GREAT interest to the words of Martin Luther King, III at a press conference in November 1997. It was then that he announced he would take over the reins of his father's old organization, the Southern Christian Leadership Conference (SCLC). I did not expect to hear ringing and defiant words from him challenging injustice and racism. This was the eloquent trademark of his dad. Forty years earlier, as head of the then fledgling SCLC, King pledged that he "would struggle and sacrifice until the walls of segregation have been fully crushed by the battering rams of justice." He more than kept that pledge.

I hoped that Martin Luther King, III might say something that would rattle a few memories of the old civil right days. While it is impossible for someone who had the crushing burden of carrying the revered name of one of the planet's true immortals to do what he did, King, III had done some things in an effort to get a bit free of his father's massive shadow. He had notched a few credentials as a human rights advocate, community activist, and political leader in Atlanta. As a member of the Board of directors of the Martin Luther King Center for Nonviolent Social Change, he was credited with inaugurating important community educational programs.

So I did expect to hear him say that he would embark on fresh campaigns against a few of the softer protest targets in the 1990s such as police abuse, the racial disparities in the criminal justice system, and the Republican-controlled Congresses' continued demolition of social programs. At the very least, I wanted some hint at which direction he intended to take his floundering organization. Although I did not hear any of that, I knew that one thing was certain. The times and challenges he faced were far different than what his father faced.

In those days black leaders had firmly staked out the moral high ground for the infant modern day civil rights movement. It was classic good versus evil. Many white Americans were sickened by the gory news scenes of baton battering racist Southern sheriffs, firehoses, police dogs, and Klan violence unleashed against peaceful black protesters. Racial segregation was considered by just about anyone and everyone who fancied themselves as decent Americans as immoral and indefensible, and the civil rights leaders were hailed as martyrs and heroes in the fight for justice.

As America unraveled in the 1960s in the anarchy of urban riots, campus takeovers, and anti-war street battles, the civil rights movement and its leaders fell apart, too. Many of them

That was a small but significant part of his life and personal lifestyle, but what about his leadership. Start with those four immortal words "I Have A Dream" belted out at the March on Washington in 1963, and eternally seared into the nation's consciousness. They have been a blessing and a curse for him in the years since. To many this indelibly dubbed King as a hopeless utopian with flights of fancy, visions of ending war, racism, and poverty but with no concrete program to come anywhere near achieving those goals. It was a simple step years after America put the flowers on him to turn him, just as was done with Malcolm X for a few months in 1992 with the mania surrounding Spike Lee's film on Malcolm, into a harmless, but badly outdated antique piece from past glory days.

Of course he was not then and is not now. In his work, largely ignored when it was published in 1966 and forgotten today, *Where Do We Go From Here: Chaos or Community?* King shifted from dreamer to problem solver. However, before examining King's ideas there are two massive caveats. Recasting the words of a historic figure to fit present times and situations must be scrupulously avoided. This type of dangerous ideological revision is self-serving and was brazenly apparent in the overblown and rancorous battles over affirmative action in the 1990s. At one point there was the weird spectacle of liberals, many blacks, Latinos, and Asian-Americans pitted against conservatives. And each jockeying hard to claim that the few stray remarks that King uttered on affirmative action before it was even called affirmative action backed liberal's embrace or conservative's hatred of it.

The second big caveat is that King can not be slotted into a neat ideological box. There is more than enough paradox and ambivalence in King's positions for black leaders and political conservatives to praise or damn him. At various times and sometimes in the same breath he harangued and embraced black militants. He advocated conservative self-help programs and socialist wealth redistribution. He applauded violent anti-colonial and national liberation movements and championed non-violent change. His solutions to many of the stupendous racial and class problems that plagued America then and torment it now are a conflicting fusion of idealism and hard nosed pragmatism. Here are some near textbook examples.

• • • • • •

The Black Family Crisis. King branded the black family "fragile, deprived and often psychopathic." This characterization accepted many of the baldest, and most vicious myths and stereotypes about black families. Yet he correctly targeted father absenteeism in the black homes as a major problem. He made the standard liberal call for more government funded job, education, and skills training programs to correct the problem. But he also recognized the importance of values, discipline, hard work, and reducing family violence to also help resolve the family crisis in many black families.

Educational Neglect. King did not believe that more funds, smaller classrooms, and better textbooks alone would solve the crisis of public education. He demanded that teachers and administrators rededicate themselves to the ideal of quality education, and for parents to get more involved in their children's education. His proposals for "educational parks," a kind of multi-faceted complex to teach basic skills and advanced studies, was the forerunner of the 1990s magnet and charter schools.

While he almost certainly would have joined with teachers unions and many mainstream black leaders in opposing school vouchers, he would have at least listened to the arguments of many poor and working-class parents that many public schools are wrecks and ruins and they, like the black middle-class and their leaders, should also have some options other than to keep their children in those schools.

Political Apathy. King believed that the right to vote and elect blacks to political office was not enough. He challenged local community groups to conduct on-going voter registration and education campaigns. He encouraged black officeholders to be "independent and assertive" in fighting for legislation to improve the plight of the black poor. He implored black political organizations and voters to build political alliances with labor, Latinos, Asians, American Indians and the white poor based on their particular needs and interests. He would probably be bitterly disappointed to see that the many in the bevy of black politicians that he and the civil rights movement made possible. Have turned a tin ear to his admonition to be "independent and assertive."

Corporate Racism. King had a four step plan to nail the rampant discrimination in hiring and promotions at corporations. First, demand more jobs and promotions; second, initiate selected buying campaigns, boycotts, and organized protests; third, conduct negotiations; fourth, monitor closely any agreement hammered out to make sure there was no backsliding by the companies once the TV cameras and the demonstrators had packed up and gone home.

Economic Empowerment. King often quipped that it was futile to integrate a lunch counter if blacks could not afford to buy a meal. He asserted that huge increases in federal funding for job and skills training programs were necessary. He also knew that government could not, should not, and would not do it all. He called for black dollar days in which blacks purchased goods and services from black businesses and deposited their savings in black owned banks.

King expected black entrepreneurs to recycle those dollars into education and social programs for the black poor. Unfortunately, he would profoundly saddened to see many of the leaders who preach the need to do that feathering their own, their organization's or their business's nest instead.

Crime and Violence. King understood that the destructive cycle of crime, drugs and violence were mighty destabilizers in many black communities. While his first priority as always was for more government supports, he also deeply believed that family values, personal responsibility, and discipline were vitally important. He pleaded with black professionals to give more of their time and money to set-up employment, educational, and recreational programs aimed at saving at-risk black youth. He would make the same plea today.

Police Abuse. King during his many campaigns for justice in the North and the South faced more abuse, harassment, and violence from police than any other major leader in the civil rights movement. He knew from personal experience the damage and devastation that this caused. He would have been the first to hit the streets in every city where police violence raised its ugly and deadly head to demand prosecutions, investigations, dismissals of officers who use excessive force, and drastic reforms in police policies and procedures.

By today's standards, King's program seems piecemeal and patchwork. Almost all of his ideas and proposals have either been implemented, tried, discarded, or discredited. But so what! King did not just dream of a new world he battled hard for it. And in this era when some black leaders believe that grabbing a photo-op or popping a sound bite is leadership, King's vision and program still seems light years ahead of anything that many of them offer or for which they are willing to fight for.

●●●●●●

If King, III is to lay any real claim to even a tiny piece of his father's leadership cloak, he will have to make a credible effort to surmount these challenges. He will also have to confront something that King did not have to confront. King had the sympathy and goodwill of millions of whites, politicians, and business leaders in the peak years of the civil rights movement. King, III does not have that. Instead he must confront the hostility and indifference of many whites to social programs, education, civil rights, and civil liberties. He will have to deal with the reality that race matters in America can no longer be framed exclusively in black and white. Latinos and Asians have become big players in the struggle for political and economic empowerment.

He will have to figure out ways to balance the competing and contradictory needs of these and other ethnic groups and patch them into a workable coalition for change. He will have to confront the mistaken conviction of many black leaders that the only place that they can and should fight racial battles are in the courts, Congress, state houses, the universities, and corporate boardrooms.

It would be grossly unfair to expect leaders such as King, III to be the charismatic, aggressive, and absolutely incorruptible champion of, and martyr for, civil rights that his father was. The times have changed too much for that. But he and other black leaders should be expected to fight the hardest they can against injustice. His and their dilemma is how to accomplish that.

III
Whither the
Congressional Black Caucus?

I AM ASKED EVERY September why I am still in Los Angeles and not at the Congressional Black Caucus's (CBC) annual gala confab in Washington D.C. The implication behind the question is that this affair is a must for anybody who is anybody. The questioners are probably right. The weekend frolic of merry making, political strategizing, and celebrity gazing is the place to be that weekend. But I think there is a better question they should ask me and themselves about the group that has designated itself to be the official political voice for the majority of African-Americans.

That question is what, if anything, Caucus members and the well-heeled, well-connected notables that flock to their gathering can do to make the CBC the strongest political voice that blacks want and need? During much of the 1990s there was a real concern by many blacks that the CBC had begun to slip badly. The concern began in grim earnest in 1994 when the Republicans assumed near total domination of the House.

They slashed congressional funds for Caucus functions, abolished the Post Office and Civil Service, and the District of Columbia Committees, which had a sizable number of black members. They reduced the size of all standing committees, costing blacks the loss of seats on several important policy-making committees, and eliminated 600 committee staff jobs, many of which were held by blacks. The slide accelerated in 1997 when the CBC suffered a crushing defeat in its battle to prevent Congress from lopping off billions in funds for social programs.

In 1997, the CBC chose outspoken California Congress-woman Maxine Waters, who has never been shy about taking the point on cutting edge social issues, to breathe the fire of legislative and more particularly public activism into the CBC. Waters's fiery political credentials could not change the fact that the CBC was squeezed hard between some harsh realities. They were: a politically tattered, Clinton, Republican intransigence, an adverse Supreme Court ruling that tossed out racial redis-tricting, the continuing assault on affirmative action and social programs, and a fragmented and often times politically coma-tose black America.

In 1998, the gossipy, trash mongering report by Independent Special Prosecutor and Republican hit man, Kenneth Starr on Clinton and Monica Lewinsky's sexual romps made matters worse for the CBC. The Republicans for a time had Clinton in full flight and made him even more shell shocked when it came to fighting hard for more black political appointees, affirmative action, and increased funds for health, education, and environmental programs.

When the Supreme Court began chipping away at race-based districts in the South in 1993, it was not the death knell for black political representation that the CBC claimed. It did mean that black candidates and incumbents in the South and other parts of the country would in future elections need much more white support to win office, and they would never be able to get that support by catering exclusively to black interests. This changing political reality was evident in 1997 when the CBC announced that it would make the battle against crime and drugs its major agenda item and cooperate wherever possible with Republicans on social issues.

To their everlasting credit, many CBC members did not grovel to the Republicans on some pressing public policy issues of the day and managed to play more than a shadow role in House fights during the mid-1990s on the budget, crime bill, NAFTA, health care, gun control, welfare reform, and environmental issues. Caucus members have even managed, on occasion, to provide the key votes that boosted the margin of victory for Democrats on a few vital pieces of legislation.

Even more to the CBC's credit it did privately lambaste Clinton in 1998 for buckling to the Republicans and hacking away funds for social programs, severely curtailing welfare programs, tepidly backing affirmative action, a much belated support of the effort to end the racial disparities in drug sentencing laws, and the virtual abandonment of his much touted "racial healing" initiatives.

And the CBC Foundation has bankrolled dozens of legal challenges to the Republican scheme to gut minority redistricting in the South. It raises thousands of dollars yearly for scholarships for students and interns.

The CBC also continued to hold hearings in selected cities throughout the 1990s on racism in the media, police abuse, health care, and education in a effort to hammer out what it considered a black agenda. One of its finest acts was to push and prod Clinton in 1999 to add millions more in federal funds for AIDS treatment and prevention programs.

But worries about the future of black political leadership still dangled precariously in the air in 1999. The National Black Leadership Roundtable is one cause for that worry. The group which is closely affiliated with the CBC is a kind of umbrella association of civil rights, business, and political leaders from around the country. It has taken solid stands on issues such as education, affirmative action, and cuts in social programs. Its brand of quiet diplomacy though, with Congress and Clinton, has left much to be desired.

For the most part it relies on a select group of scholars and experts to develop reports and position papers on issues. There appears to be little or no effort to inform the black public and involve community activists in its political actions. They are left almost completely in the dark on how their efforts translate into legislation that directly impacts on black communities. In the absence of this feedback and involvement, the impression is that the Roundtable leaders spend much if not the bulk of their time and resources to the narrow and self-preserving task of electing more black democrats to office, and making sure that those already there stay there, i.e. themselves.

Many black politicians dread hearing the word "elitist" applied to them. They, like every other politician breathing, solemnly swear that they listen to what the people say and act on what they want. They tell themselves and the public that everything they do is done on behalf of their constituents. It is. And it is not. There is a considerable amount of good legislation they propose and even occasionally get passed that deal with problems and needs of poor and working class blacks.

This does not alter the fact that the American political system is a self-protective, clubby, and chummy ball game. As the consummate political insiders, they spend most of their time with each other. This undergirds their self-assigned role as experts in and arbiters of the inner craft of American politics. They are accustomed to the unchallenged and unquestioned brandishing of power. They jealously hoard what they view as their sacred right to make all final decisions on proposing laws and supporting public policy they deem important. More often than not those laws and policies boost middle-class blacks and corporate special interests rather than poor and working-class blacks.

• • • • • •

Nowhere was this more graphically evident than when the CBC tied itself tightly to Clinton's often times frayed coat tails throughout both of his terms in the 1990s. They virtually gave him a free ride on many of the most critical social issues to blacks, minorities, and the poor. But why? There are several answers to this question. They are Democrats and so are most blacks. They, like most politicians, read the opinion polls and they knew that Clinton was wildly popular with many blacks.

They remembered the grotesque Reagan years of the 1980s, and the equally grotesque political machinations of Republicans Newt Gringrich and Mississippi Senator Trent Lott who dominated the House and Senate during the Clinton years of the 1990s. They were convinced that Clinton was the only politician that stood between them and total doom for African-Americans at the hands of the Republicans. They were totally dependent on the political and financial largesse of the Democratic Party for political patronage, support, and assorted party favors. They fervently believed that they could do more good by silently working to get good legislation through Congress than raising their voices in protest.

These are all perfectly valid answers for the CBC's near blind public faith in Clinton. Yet they still can not tap dance around the fact that when the Clinton legacy is assessed it will show that Clinton did the kind of social damage to blacks that Reagan and Bush, only talked and dreamed about doing. And the CBC publicly said nothing and did nothing about them.

Racial Stereotypes. Following the verdict in the O.J. Simpson criminal trial in 1995, Clinton asked white Americans to "respect" the jury's decision, not accept it. This not-so-subtle distinction reinforced the false belief of many white Americans that the predominantly black jury acquitted Simpson on the basis of race rather than the prosecution's horribly bungled job of presenting its case, let alone proving it. Clinton apparently had much on his mind and maybe some of his own residual anger over the decision when in a speech immediately following the Million Man March held in 1995, he repeated these ancient stereotypes

"Violence for white people too often comes with a black face."

(**Fact.** The majority of violent crime is committed by other whites. The mass murders and shootings of whites by whites at Columbine High School in Colorado in 1999 and a rash of shootings at other high schools of whites by whites in 1998 and 1999 should have finally buried that myth for Clinton.)

"It isn't racist for whites to say they don't understand why people put up with...drugs being sold in the schools or in the open."

(**Fact.** The overwhelming majority of drug users and abusers in America are white, and more often than not, middle-class males and females who live in the comfy suburbs or penthouses.)

"It's not racist to assert that the culture of welfare dependency can't be broken unless there is first more personal responsibility."

(**Fact.** The media delighted in the 1990s in trotting out poster women pictures of blacks in its news features and stories on welfare queens, cheats, and roustabouts. The biggest single group on the dole is and always has been whites.)

When Clinton uttered these falsehoods as gospel was he inadvertently blaming and scapegoating blacks for America's social ills?

Racial Healing. With much fanfare Clinton established a high-brow racial panel in 1997 to recommend ways to heal the racial divide in America. But from the start Clinton made it clear that he would not put any political zest behind whatever proposals the panel scrounged up to deal with the divide. As it turned out they came up with nothing earth shattering.

They proposed more support for affirmative action, better police-community relations, and cosmetic reforms in the criminal justice system. The panel was concerned with finding the quickest, easiest, and cheapest way to attain some sort of vague, poorly defined, and ultimately mythical racial harmony that would not disturb fundamental power relations between the rich and the powerful and the minority poor.

If this was not disappointing enough, Clinton foot-dragged for months before he publicly decided to print the panel's findings and recommendations. Much of the delay was due to wrangling by some among his inner circle of advisors who begged him not to print the report for fear it might anger whites.

Affirmative Action. After conservative Republicans claimed that white males were losing ground to minorities, Clinton in 1995 promised to end abuses in federal government affirmative action programs. He was as good as his word. Many federal government agencies either dropped or let lapse various minority business support programs that in the past had given many blacks, minorities, and women a giant boost in private and government contracting.

Even as Clinton began his stealth dismantling of these programs, there was never any federal mandate that forced contractors to replace white workers with minorities and women. There were never more than a handful of government set aside programs in procurement and contracting, and that the Supreme Court's decision in the Paradise case in 1987 was the only case that explicitly upheld quotas. It applied almost exclusively to police and fire departments and even then it did not prevent these departments from hiring whites.

The issue of affirmative action throughout the 1990s inflamed many whites and some blacks and other non-blacks and was used by cynical politicians to grab votes. Clinton bought into this nonsense and mania, and by doing so put one more nail in the coffin of affirmative action.

Welfare. Reagan and Bush promised to end welfare as America knew it. They could not. Clinton could and did in 1997. All three presidents fanned these racial and sexual myths about welfare. It encouraged dependency, cheating, laziness, and out of wedlock births. It was a massive drain on the taxpayers. And the best lie of all, the recipients were mostly poor black women.

When welfare programs got the big ax, Clinton and the Republicans were not willing to spend more than a pittance for job and skills training, education, health, or child care programs. This would guarantee that the next time the economy goes through its cyclical bust and plant and store lay-offs, cutbacks, and downsizing begin with real mercilessness, those same welfare recipients that managed to get low end jobs are not unceremoniously heaped on the streets this time with no where to turn for help.

Crime. In 1994, Clinton rammed through Congress the most wasteful and punitive crime bill in American history, the Omnibus Crime Bill. It drained funds for drug rehab and prevention programs, social services, youth employment, recreation, and job training programs. It added scores of new death penalty provisions to federal law and shoveled out billions exclusively for more police and prisons. In 1998, the U.S. Sentencing Commission recommended to Congress that the harsh sentences for crack cocaine use and sale given to mostly black and Latino offenders and the light as a feather hand slap sentences for powdered cocaine use and sale given to mostly white offenders be modified, not eliminated.

Clinton had never said a word about this ridiculous double standard in the enforcement of the drug laws. After much public pressure and a mountain of evidence that record numbers of young blacks and Latinos were being locked up in America's prisons due to the racial double-standard in the drug laws and with no end in sight to drug use or sale, Clinton changed his mind and agreed to back the change. When Congress said no to the Commission and Clinton on changing the law. The president went quietly into the night without a peep of protest about it.

● ● ● ● ● ●

CBC members and all of Clinton's black Democratic defenders, when pressed about their impassioned defense of him during his terms in office, shot back that he appointed blacks to high administrative positions, supported minority redistricting, took tough action on the rash of black church burnings, spoke up on police abuse and racial profiling, and fought to have a more equitable Census count. He did. These were no-risk, high return political actions. He raised his voice in protest only after there was a groundswell of public indignation, outrage, and protest.

The appointments of blacks were to high profile positions, with relatively little major policy making power and authority. The major power positions in any president's cabinet are Attorney General, Secretary of State, Secretary of the Treasury, White House Counsel, and National Security Advisor. Blacks held none of those positions. He did not fight for his nominee, Lani Guinier, to head the Justice Department's Civil Rights Division in 1993, and quickly dumped Surgeon General Jocelyn Elders in 1997 after she got mild flack from conservative Republicans. Even before the Lewinsky scandal in 1998, Clinton had begun to backslide in appointing blacks to judgeships, administration, and cabinet posts when Congressional Republicans made it clear that they would hold any and all of his black appointees hostage to their Dark Ages political whims.

Clinton had to oppose Southern redistricting and the anti-quated method of the census count. It would have meant the potential loss of Democratic seats in the districts that were reconfigured due to the Supreme Court decision. A more accurate census would have meant that the millions of blacks, Latinos, and American Indians that the census routinely undercounts every decade would be far more likely to vote Democratic than Republican.

To chalk the CBC's political slippage in the mid-1990s up to political kowtowing to Clinton, obstructionist Republicans, or to vested interest in maintaining its own political power is too easy. The blame in part lay in the near permanent invisibility of large numbers of blacks from the voting booths, in part to the muted reaction of many blacks to crisis issues such as racial hate crimes, welfare reform, deterioration of many public schools, the wipe-out of social programs, the disastrous racial disparities in the criminal justice system, and in part to the CBC's own shaky political accommodationism.

This sends the ominous message that if many blacks do not care what politicians do or say about their interests, then why should black elected officials beat their heads against the wall to defend those interests? There are more than a few black elected officials who would be more than content to heed that message.

With Clinton out of the White House and the prospect of a Republican hard-line conservative George W. Bush as president in 2000, millions of African-Americans will desperately need a strong legislative voice raised in defense of their interests AND a strong public voice to politically energize people into action. The CBC then would do well to remember its oft repeated motto of no "permanent friends, no permanent enemies, only permanent interests." This is the only way that they will become the permanent political voice that blacks must have to advance in this society.

IV
The Tattered Tale of Two Icons

I QUICKLY REALIZED THAT what had started out as a relaxing evening at a local jazz club in Hollywood back in the mid-1970s quickly became an annoying experience for me sitting at the table next to Bill Cosby. He had barely taken his seat when people began parading to his table waving their business cards and shouting one scheme or another in his face. They bumped and jostled me as they passed with no thought of apology. This incident happened several years before NBC's *The Cosby Show*, had enshrined him as America's number one dad, and made him one of America's wealthiest men.

That evening Cosby was already a hot commodity. He was the first black to co-star in a network TV series I Spy, the national pitchman for Jello-O and Coca Cola, and a popular nightclub comedy performer. Cosby took the intrusions in stride. He smiled at each supplicant, shook their hands, took their business cards, and listened patiently to their ploys.

As I watched the spectacle at his table I suddenly felt intense empathy for him. He was a public figure, indeed many saw him as a black spokesperson, who could not relax and enjoy a quiet night out. Once or twice when I caught his eye, he nodded at me, faintly smiled, and shrugged, as if to say, this is the price I must pay for being a celebrity and a black spokesperson.

Two decades later, Cosby was still paying that price. He was voted by an MCI Father's Day Poll, in *USA Today* in 1996 as the most memorable TV dad of all time. And he was at or near the top of *Forbes* magazine's annual list of the richest entertainers in America, with his net worth at an estimated $300 million. He was so idolized that the FBI once enlisted him in its national publicity campaign to find missing children. Cosby had seemingly smashed all the barriers to African-American progress in entertainment and society. The *New York Times* called him "The black face that's a mirror for everybody." He had become a mythic icon and America's universal symbol of hope and accomplishment.

That all suddenly paled when Cosby got the shattering news that his son, Ennis, had been murdered. The public reaction came as close as America comes to a national day of mourning that is traditionally reserved after the deaths of Presidents and revered public figures.

His prodigious achievements fueled the delusionary belief by many Americans that money and fame can prevent black icons from being toppled from their pedestal. It can not.

••••••

Cosby certainly did not share that delusion. He knew that wealthy, and famous black men who are routinely lauded, lionized, and coronated as spokesmen for black America are fragile. They are often only one innocent misstep away from being marginalized, neutralized, and jostled from the spotlight. He said as much at the Academy of TV Arts and Sciences Hall of Fame induction ceremonies in 1992. The star-studded crowd chuckled at the one liners delivered by its principal inductee, Cosby.

The laughter stopped when he turned serious and accused white film and TV writers of "massacring" the black image on screen. The indictment seemed ironic coming from the man whom America enshrined as its most treasured media figure. It was doubly ironic because it pointed to much of the media and public's schizoid nature. It made Cosby, a black man and a leader who was the ultimate in role models and the symbol of all that is good and wholesome in America, and at the same time it happily stamped black men with the crime-drugs-violence-derelict label.

Even amidst the hyper-adulation of Cosby and the colossal ratings for the Cosby show in the 1980s, there were warning signs in those years that Cosby was not immune from racial problems. He was found guilty of assaulting a white photographer on evidence that pretty much amounted to the photographer's word. His movies *Leonard Part VI*, *Ghost Dad*, and the *Cosby Mystery Series* were flops. Critics attributed their failure to lousy plots and poor writing. In truth, the public winced at accepting Cosby in anything other than the comic role traditionally reserved for blacks in TV.

Even the media that patted itself on the back for its deferential treatment of Cosby after his son's murder still made sly references to Cosby's early misfortunes with Ennis and reminded the public of his well-publicized estrangement from his daughter, Erin, after her drug problems. Cosby, sensing the danger from a media trained to sniff out scandal, pleaded for it to act "dignified." This momentarily blunted the media feeding frenzy.

Cosby then made the bombshell confession that beginning in the 1970s he had a rendezvous with another woman (i.e. an extra marital affair) twenty years ago. He probably felt compelled to reveal this after the arrest of a twenty-year-old woman who claimed to be his illegitimate daughter for attempting to extort $40 million from him. She and a partner were convicted in 1997, and in a humiliating legal slap at the prosecution—and Cosby—were released on a judicial technicality in May 1999 after barely serving one year behind bars.

The tiny cracks in the pedestal that he rested comfortably on for so many years turned into a deep fault when his wife, Camille Cosby, had the audacity, presumably with Bill's full approval, to suggest in the aftermath of the trial and conviction of her son's murderer that he was poisoned by American racism. She did not stop there. She also ripped the cover off of America's great falsehood that blacks commit the majority of violent crimes. They do not. Whites commit just as many if not more violent crimes than blacks. This sent the professional black baiters into a froth. They pounded her, and by extension hubby Bill, from pillar to post in print, on the airwaves, and in parlor conversations. Their fury at her was so intense that for a moment some wondered whether they believed she was an even bigger criminal for daring to speak the truth than was her son's murderer for committing the homicide?

That again pointed to one of Cosby's problems. Many Americans have a nasty habit of turning against their black icons at the first hint of scandal, or their icon's first utterance of candid words about racism that they feel exceeds the bounds of propriety. The black image that Cosby accused those white writers of "massacring" it seemed, for the briefest of moments, turned into a dooming self-prophecy for him.

• • • • • • •

If Cosby was the victim of subtle and nasty digs when personal misfortune struck, there was nothing subtle about the way the pack of political enemies struck at Clinton's Commerce Secretary Ron Brown in life and even in death. In the days after his tragic death in a plane crash in Croatia in 1996 scores of political leaders called Brown a talented, selfless, dedicated public servant who rose to the pinnacle of power and success through hard work and dedication. Some went further and implied that Brown's accomplishment proved that racism was no barrier for blacks willing to work and sacrifice to attain success. They used Brown to feed yet another fantasy that America has become a race-neutral society where individuals are judged on their talent and ability not skin color.

The hypocrisy in this was enough to make anyone, who

knew what Brown's enemies did and said about him when he was breathing, vomit. Many of the same individuals who praised Brown after his death denounced him as a crook and demanded that Clinton fire him and a grand jury indict him when he was alive. When partisan Republicans accused Brown of financial improprieties in the mid 1990s, Attorney General Janet Reno immediately appointed Miami lawyer, David Pearson, as independent special counsel to probe his political and financial dealings.

The investigation was relentless and wide-ranging. The press gleefully pawned off every bit of gossip, innuendo and rumor about Brown's alleged shady dealings as fact. He was accused of reaping huge profits from the Belle Haven Apartments in Prince Georges County, Maryland. They claimed that the owners had deliberately neglected repairs to cut costs and increase profits.

He was accused of being an influence peddler for using his office to snare lucrative contracts with the Public Employees Benefit Services Corporation. He was accused of using insider trader information to bag profits from stocks in the Corridor Broadcasting Corporation. He was accused of failing to disclose a mortgage loan.

He was accused of buttonholing a friend to pay off his personal debts. Brown denied the allegations. Investigators never found, or at least never publicly revealed, any concrete evidence of any criminal wrongdoing by Brown or that he misused his office for personal gain.

Washington insiders are certainly aware that many political

officials use their political contacts to increase their financial investments and political influence. They are routinely applauded by the media, praised by the public and courted by business leaders for their political skill and savvy. The difference is that they are politically well-connected white males. Brown was not. As special counsel Pearson continued to dig into his finances, the rumors, innuendoes, and accusations about Brown continued to fly. The *Wall Street Journal* branded him the "Beltway wheeler dealer." The *Washington Post* flatly claimed that Brown was "driven by money."

The *Post, New York Times, Los Angeles Times,* and *Wall Street Journal* stepped up the attack on him. Here's a sampling of their editorial slants:

"Now Ron Brown's investigation" (*Washington Post*)
"Mr. Clinton's Ron Brown problem" (*New York Times*)
"Mr. Brown's woes" (*Christian Science Monitor*)
"End the dodging on Ron Brown" (*New York Times*)

In a front page "exposés" of alleged Brown wrongdoings, the *Los Angeles Times* zeroed in on Brown's involvement with the Belle Haven Apartments. A Brown associate refuted the charges in a letter. It was buried in the letters section of the Op-Ed page. Meanwhile *Time* magazine confidently predicted that Brown's days were beginning to be numbered.

Even before Pearson began his investigation in 1995, twenty-two GOP legislators demanded that he resign. Some used Brown's troubles to justify their repeated call for eliminating the Commerce Department. If Brown had lived, almost certainly more Republicans (and Democrats) would have jumped on the dump Brown bandwagon.

Even his death did not free him from the heavy taint of scandal. Pearson announced that he would shift the probe to Brown's son, Michael and his business partner, Yolanda Hill. This appeared to be nothing but a thinly disguised effort to keep the spotlight on Brown as a prime suspect. Long before this, Brown Sr.'s political stock had slipped badly and his effectiveness as a black leader had seriously eroded. More than a few blacks quietly and privately raised questions about his credibility. The stacks of political and media generated innuendoes, gossip, and character attacks had more than done the job on him.

••••••

Clinton publicly stood by Brown during the time he was under fire. The betting odds among political insiders was that Brown would have probably gotten the boot if Clinton were reelected in 1996. Clinton was re-elected but Brown was dead by then.

Brown was a highly skilled administrator and a talented political and business leader. He made a major effort to increase job and promotion opportunities for minorities and women within the Commerce Department. He increased government funds and programs for minority businesses and economic development projects in local communities. He was a solid and effective role model of success and achievement for African-Americans. His loss was deeply mourned by all who understood his importance.

He understood that despite his personal success he was still a black leader under an intense racial looking glass. And that no matter how much success he attained as businessman and political leader, to some he would always be Ron Brown the "Beltway wheeler-dealer."

During much of the 1980s and 1990s the names Ron Brown and Bill Cosby were the emblems of black success, talent, wealth, power, and fame in America. When many thought of black leaders and spokespersons their names were also among the first to be uttered. Yet in life for Cosby, and life and in death for Brown, their money and fame notwithstanding, they were never more than one misstep or misdeed, real or imagined, away from being seen as damaged goods as black spokesmen and leaders, and worse, as badly tattered icons.

V
Why Speak for Black Women

I THOUGHT IT WOULD BE AN ISSUE that many black women would be anxious to discuss. The issue is the punishing number of black women that are behind bars in America. More than half of the 140,000 women jailed in 1998 were black women. Eighty percent of them were mothers and seventy percent were single parents with small children. More of them than ever were doing time because of the drug crackdown, the hard public mood on crime, racial disparities in the criminal justice system, and poverty.

In 1998, in California and several other states, for the first time in American history, black women were being locked up in nearly the same numbers as white men. They have almost single-handedly in the past decade powered the spectacular expansion of the gender end of the prison-industrial complex.

I fully expected that the treatment of mostly poor, and

working class black women would prompt the leaders of the NAACP, SCLC, CORE, and the Urban League, women's groups, the major black women's organizations such as the National Council of Negro Women as well as hundreds of local black women groups, sororities, and associations to take up their cause. I thought they would be eager to hammer on public officials to increase resources, services, and propose legislation to stem the tide of black female incarceration.

I was wrong. At the close of 1998, I had not heard or read where any of these groups, or the hundreds of national and local black female elected officials had proposed firm policy initiatives to deal with the crisis of black women prisoners. Their silence became less of a puzzle when I realized two things. The first is that the popular myth is that black women are not considered physical threats and economic competitors to white males as black men. Black leaders and organizations like most Americans are deluged with newspaper reports, TV specials and academic studies on at risk or endangered black males. They see black men in crisis. They do not see that black women are in crisis, too.

The second reason is that many of the traditional black women's organizations and black female leaders are middle-class, business and professional persons. Their sights are set on advancing their careers in corporations, moving up in the professions, and establishing more businesses. The rash of black magazines that cater exclusively to career-tracked, upwardly mobile black women are choked with stories and features on health and fitness, lifestyles, celebrity gossip, relationships, travel, fashions, and of course, how to get rich, rich, rich.

They are vaguely uneasy at the plight of poor black women that are homeless on the streets, on welfare rolls, and behind prison bars. These are problems that are remote and distant to some. To others who themselves have been in that situation, or who have relatives or friends that are, they are trying to put those hard times behind them, and deny that they are still major problems. To others poor black women are a shame and embarrassment.

• • • • • •

The class and gender outrages still suffered by many black poor women send shivers through many middle-class black women. They realize that their plight could easily be their plight, too. The truth is that it often is and one only has to take even the most cursory look at the damage that gender and racial stereotypes have wreaked on all black women to see that.

Black women were never accorded the protection and "privileges" of white women in America. There is bitter truth to the old line that the only time black women are ever called ladies is when they are cleaning ladies. Slavery distorted and narrowed the gender lines between black men and women. Black women were treated as commodities to be beaten, worked, raped, and abused to boost the profit power and sexual pleasure of the slavemaster.

During the segregation era, black women were constant targets of violence. Between 1891 and 1921, forty-five black women (known) were lynched, shot, burned or beaten to death by white mobs. Several of the victims were teenagers. Several were pregnant. When a white mob obliterated the all-black town of Rosewood, Florida in 1921, black women were the first murdered. Hundreds more were forced to flee in terror.

Most black women did not live the mythical Ozzie and Harriet lifestyle of housewife, nurturer, and caregiver. The majority of black women were employed outside the home as domestics, cooks, cleaning and laundry workers. They were low paid, unskilled workers in plants, factories, and on the farms.

The heavy dose of racial and gender stereotypes that continue to take a heavy toll on black women, middle-class and poor, rests solidly on stubbornly engrained myths.

Image Assault. While much of the media enshrined the stereotypes of black men as lazy, violent, crime prone, sexual menaces; black women were typed much the same way. The stereotypes were permanently burned into the minds of many Americans in ads, films, and early sit-coms. In *Amos 'n Andy*, Widow Parker was a scheming gold-digger, greedily on the prowl for men and money. Madam Queen was a sexually loose, con artist. Sapphire was shrill, domineering, and bossy. Mama was boozy, ignorant, and crude.

In *Gone With the Wind* and popular product advertisements, Beaulah and Aunt Jemima were depicted as fat, bandanna wearing eternally suffering and patient earth mothers (to whites). The black female image was trashed in the blaxploitation films of the 1970s and the sit-coms, gangster, and gender bashing films of the 1990s.

Feminization of Poverty. In 1999, more than one out of three black women had incomes below the poverty level. One out of seven was unemployed. One out of two was a single parent. One out of three was employed in a low wage, semi, or unskilled service or retail jobs. One out of three did not complete high school.

The shooting death of Margaret Mitchell, a middle-aged, homeless woman in Los Angeles in May 1999 by a Los Angeles police officer spotlighted another calamity for black women, homelessness. African-Americans make up more than half of the homeless in America and black women make up a significant number of those dumped on the streets.

Devalued Lives. The shooting by three Riverside police officers of Tyisha Miller in December 1998 and the shooting of Mitchell drew national media attention and much public outrage. The shootings were deadly proof that black women, like black men, are at serious risk from deadly violence other than from police bullets.

Between 1980 and 1985, the number of black women murdered exceeded the number of American soldiers killed in Vietnam in 1967, a peak year of the fighting. By 1990, homicide was the number one killer of young black females. A black woman was ten times likelier to be raped than a white woman and slightly more likely to be the victim of domestic violence than a white woman. The media often magnifies and sensationalizes crimes by black men against white women and ignores or downplays crimes against black women.

Violent death is only one of the life threatening perils facing black women, they are double, triple and even quadruple times more likely to suffer breast cancer, die during pregnancy, and be stricken with AIDS/HIV disease than white women. When they are afflicted they are far less likely to have adequate access to adequate medical care and treatment than white women.

Welfare and Single Parenthood. In 1999, nearly two out of three welfare recipients lived in a suburb or rural area, stay on welfare less than four years, had no more than two children, and were white. When jobs, skills training, and child care are available welfare recipients grab them.

In the heyday of welfare in the 1970s and early 1980s, there was never any evidence that poor black women made babies in order to live luxuriously at state expense. Even if they wanted to, no state ever had maximum benefit levels high enough to allow recipients to exist at the official federal poverty level. The national average monthly welfare payout was never more than $400.

The twin myth still persists that black teens have a monopoly on "illegitimate" or out-of-wedlock births. They do not. During the 1990s the typical single mother was a white, affluent, well-educated working woman. Sixty percent of out-of-wedlock births were to white women and seventy percent to women older than age 20. The number of black unmarried teen girls having babies, though still disproportionately high, has sharply dropped since 1992.

Prison. The draconian cuts by many states in welfare benefits as well as tougher eligibility requirements shoved many black women into economic destitution or to the streets. Racially discriminatory drug sentencing laws, racially biased judges and juries, media sensationalized black female violence, the hard nosed public mood on crime and drugs, and the feminization of poverty created a fresh crisis within the legal system. Black women are seven times more likely to be jailed than white women. By 1998, three out of one hundred black women were in prison, on probation, or parole.

The majority of their children are warehoused in foster homes and institutions. Deprived of constant parental care and nurturing, many of these children are virtually doomed to perpetuate the cycle of crime-arrest-incarceration.

•••••••

For a brief moment in 1997 there was a glimmer of hope and promise that a handful of grassroots leaders had finally stepped forth to deal with the woes that had mounted high on the doorsteps of many black women, particularly poor and working class black women. Two women alarmed at the assault, and indifference of black elected officials, the lack of programs and initiatives to deal with them, and disgusted at the inaction of the traditional black advocacy organizations and women's groups decided to take matters into their own hands. They organized the Million Woman March in Philadelphia in October 1997.

They faced the open hostility of city officials and defections from local women groups and leaders who initially were favorable to the March. They ignored the taunts and put downs from some black men and women who warned that it was silly to try to take such an action without the backing of a name organization or leader behind it. They did not really expect it or solicit it. They knew that given the frosty attitude of black leaders to maverick grassroots movements initiated by the poor and working class they were unlikely to get it anyway. They were right. At first they received no endorsements from any black organizations or elected officials, no offers of help or support, and almost no publicity from black radio stations, or newspapers.

Even black America's stoutest public issues warrior California Congresswoman Maxine Waters was initially wary and voiced many suspicions about the leadership and the purpose of the March. After some haggling she finally accepted an invitation to speak. Dorothy Height president of the National Council of Negro Women also came and spoke.

The March organizers belatedly extended invitations to civil rights movement living legends Rosa Parks and Coretta Scott King. Both begged off due to "prior commitments." The organizers were forced to reach all the way to South Africa to get Winnie Mandela as a speaker. She turned out to be the event's only real major draw.

After the March had drawn the huge throngs of working class women, some black leaders finally took note. In his President's letter shortly after the March, NAACP executive director Kweisi Mfume praised the March and insisted that the NAACP had supported it. This seemed like more of an after thought than anything else since there was no public acknowledgment or indication by the March organizers that NAACP leaders were anywhere to be seen at the March or rendered any active support to them before the March.

The March organizers pounded out a no-frills platform and program that zeroed in directly on the problems of poor and working-class, black women such as more and better health facilities, emphasis on preventive health care, more resources for child care, improved public education, rites of passage centers, and bolstering family relations. They made the center-piece of their program the issue that not one mainstream black organization and women's group had made more than a nodding mention of and that is the plight of black women in prison, and those released from prison. They called for greater support for low-cost medical services, job and skills training, education programs, child care, and drug treatment programs to aid women in prison and on their release from prison to insure that they do not land there again.

The March organizers momentarily had the last laugh when nearly one million women heeded their plea and jammed the Benjamin Parkway in Philadelphia. The euphoria of the women was intoxicating. They vowed to keep the spirit alive in their communities. But many women treated the March like a rock concert or revival, basking in the glow and spirit of sisterhood. They hugged, they weeped, they danced, they sang, and they told themselves that this was the culminating symbol of black female power.

Long before the last speaker had finished, the euphoria that many of the women had felt over sisters bonding had begun to dissipate. Many of them grumbled that the March seemed to lack any purpose and direction, and was disorganized and disconnected. Many drifted away muttering to themselves and those around them, okay now what?

This was the same question and problem that thousands of men at the Million Man March in 1995 wondered and asked. The only way that this deflation and inertia could have been avoided was to have had strong, functioning local organizing committees well in place LONG BEFORE the March. These committees would not exist solely as a one shot effort to plan and organize the March but to plan and organize community actions, devise programs, and work with local organizations.

The aim of the organizers should have been to make sure that these committees stayed in place AFTER the March ended. That did not happen. When the women's tears of joy dried up, the same problems that propelled them to Philadelphia were still there and cried just as loudly for action as before. The local black organizations, neighborhood groups, block clubs, PTAs, churches, and social service agencies in every city they came from still begged for more black women to get involved with their programs and activities. That included many of the women that hugged and celebrated sister power in Philadelphia.

Still, the March was not a wasted effort. It made many women see even more clearly that there are vast numbers of women who care about the plight of poor and black working class women, and that they do not have to wait for traditional black organizations and women's groups to do the job for them. They can be their own leaders and advocates for change. Dorothy Height got it right when she told the throng, "We don't want anyone to tell us what are problems are, we want to tell them." The problem was and is that the "Them" is still many black leaders.

••••••

Black women, especially poor and working class black women, are blamed for the crisis problems of welfare, sexual decadence, teen pregnancy, family instability, and increasingly crime, violence, and drugs. They are accused of emasculating and taking jobs away from black men. Their special needs and problems are ignored by many feminists and women's organizations. But they are disgracefully ignored by black leaders and organizations, and even more particularly by black women's groups who too often purposely or unwittingly distance themselves from these women. The growth industry in black female stereotypes and the steep ascent in social and physical assaults on black women has hardened public attitudes on race, made black women the scapegoats for many of the dire problems in American society, and created damaging rifts between poor and working class black women and traditional black leaders.

Sisterhood may be a powerful slogan but when it comes to the predicament of many black women as far as many black leaders, men and women, are concerned, it is just that, a slogan.

VI
Black Politicians:
Lost, Stolen, and Strayed

I WAS GLAD AND SAD when Clinton's former agricultural secretary Mike Espy was acquitted on bribery charges in 1998. I was glad because he did not take the cheap and easy way out to win his legal victory by claiming that as the first African-American to head the Agriculture Department he was the victim of a racially-motivated plot by Republicans to discredit African-American political leaders. Before his trial some expected him to play the race card. It is understandable why they would expect that since some black politicians when facing heavy legal fire have quickly latched on to the issue of race to deflect attention from their crimes.

One has only to remember that during the 1990s former Illinois congressman Mel Reynolds screamed racism when he was indicted, tried, and convicted of sexual assault charges.

Washington, D.C. Mayor Marion Barry screamed racism when he was indicted, tried, and convicted on a drug charge. California Congressman Walter Tucker screamed racism when he was convicted of bribery charges.

Even though their knee jerk cry of white persecution did not fly, they played the odds and reminded blacks that Reagan's Justice Department initiated dozens of corruption probes against black elected officials during the 1980s. Given the Reagan administration's open hostility to civil rights and social programs, it is easy to believe that some of these cases walked, if not outright crossed over, the thin line between legitimate concern with bagging lawbreakers and racially-motivated political harassment of black leadership.

Yet I was sad that Espy had wound up in a court docket. I had to temper my joy over his triumph with regret that being there at all further tarnished the image of black political leaders. If this seems like a harsh imposition that black politicians be cleaner in their political dealings than white politicians, there is a reason. Black politicians have a special duty to the black communities. Many blacks view them not as politicians, but as leaders and advocates. They look to them to represent their interests and to confront institutional power. When they take bribes, or are even accused of taking them, they betray the trust of African-Americans.

Many black politicians are not newcomers to politics. Most are long-term Democratic party veterans who know well the political ropes. Espy was a three-term congressman from Mississippi before he took the agricultural post in 1993. If it had been shown that he had actually taken brides or committed other illegal acts, then he did it because he thought he could get away with it, and not out of any babe-in-the woods naiveté or innocence.

Espy did not dispute the charge that he took gifts from friends and businesses but insisted that they were given and accepted out of friendship, and not in return for political favors. Though a jury believed his claim that still means he felt that his office and position conferred upon him a special privilege and that gift taking came with the turf.

The failed prosecution of Espy proved that he was not a victim of white persecution or a corrupt politician. It also proved that the political dealings of black politicians will and should be watched and scrutinized just as closely as those of white politicians.

••••••

When black politicians take bribes and assorted favors, and then lie about it they do more than sully the image of black leaders. They also make it much harder for blacks to have and retain confidence in them. When that happens this diminishes their political power and influence. It creates distrust and dissension among black voters. This in turn makes it more difficult for blacks to win and hold political office. The vanishing of more and more blacks from the political radar scope is especially noticeable in California, the nation's most populous and politically influential state. The failure of a well-heeled black politician, Elihu Harris, to win election to a state assembly seat from Oakland in 1999 could be a bad signal of what is in store for black elected officials who are not attuned to their constituent's needs.

On paper Harris should have been a cinch to win an assembly seat in a special election in black majority Oakland in 1999. He was a former mayor of the city, a long-term assemblyman who represented the area, and one of the state's most respected black politicians. His major opponent was a white attorney. Yet Harris failed to get a majority of the vote and was forced into a run-off against of all things a Green Party candidate.

The Greens are a lightly regarded third party with almost no political influence in any state, that is until the race against Harris. In the ultimate indignity he was beaten. The major reason for his defeat was that most African-American voters in Oakland found him uninspiring and his program irrelevant to their needs. On election day, they stayed at home. His defeat tells why many African-American leaders are engaged in much hand wringing and soul searching over the sinking political fortunes of blacks in that state's politics. It is also a cautionary tale for blacks in other states and cities where they once held mayorships and many local offices.

When the California state legislature met in 1996, there were 10 black state representatives. By 2000, that number had dipped to six and they were all represented in districts in a narrow band in Los Angeles County. At the same time that blacks were jetting backwards politically in state politics, Latinos were barreling ahead. They had increased their number of seats in the state legislature to twenty-four in 1999 and held some of the most visible positions in state government. If the current population projections hold up, Latinos will be the dominant minority in America by the year 2010 and the overwhelming majority in California long before then. Their political future in California and other states was beginning to shine brighter than the sun in the Sahara Desert in July.

The sharp plunge in the political bounty of blacks in state politics is blamed on voter apathy, alienation, inner city population drops, suburban integration, and displacement by Latinos and increasingly Asians who some claim have far more cohesion and political savvy than blacks. These are factors that have contributed to the free-fall in the number of black elected officials. There is another reason for the crash dive that many blacks are too horrified to admit. It is called class division.

There are no longer just two Americas in conflict, one black and one white. There is also the conflict between the prospering and expanding black middle class and an increasingly desperate and destitute black poor. This has opened a political rift as wide as the Grand Canyon. The issue of school vouchers which an awesome number of poor and working blacks say they want and the election of white mayors in even majority or near majority black cities are foreboding signs of the time.

The election of Jerry Brown as mayor in Oakland was an even more foreboding hint of this in 1998. Black voters bought his pitch that he would not dip his hand in the till and fight harder for more jobs, better public schools, and municipal services, and against crime, than the black candidates he ran against and trounced.

This shift in black interests should have been the herald to all current or future hopeful black elected officials that guilt tainted appeals for black solidarity and voter registration caravans and buses into black neighborhoods are not going to make blacks dash to the polls to vote for politicians they feel have, or will, fail them. That attitude might change if and when black politicians who want to win or stay in office find a way to reconnect with the black poor, and customize an agenda that can motivate, inspire, and renew their belief that black office holders care about their interests, too. Black elected officials and those blacks who desire to be officials and therefore leaders must also expand their agenda to include building coalitions and alliances with Latinos and Asians.

• • • • • •

They will also have to broaden their vision to see that there are two other possible ways to increase or preserve the political gains of blacks. The first is through independent bloc voting. That is not the same thing as a third party or an all-black party. Those are pipe dreams. During the 20th Century the Afro-American Party, the Negro Political Union, the Freedom Now Party, the Black Panther Party, both the original one in the South and the gun toting one in the North, in 1966, and the National Independent Black Party were all efforts to resurrect a black party. They all crashed against the hard bedrock of ram-rod rigid black loyalty to the Republicans and Democrats, political opportunism, fear, and conservatism. Independent bloc voting, however, is a viable stepping stone toward increasing political power and the number of black officeholders.

This means that black politicians must reach out to the poor, devise an action program, and do consistent and sustained grassroots community mobilizing inside and outside the Democratic party. The Rainbow Coalition, despite its mammoth flaws, and failed promise, was a good model of how to creatively use the political process to energize large numbers of people. The Coalition's aims were to increase black voting strength, gain concessions from the Democrats, put more black candidates into political office. It launched voter registration and political mobilization campaigns. It capitalized on the nationally recognized name and prestige of its titular leader Jesse Jackson.

The second way to increase black political power is a way that sends many black politicians into a delirium of fright. They must try to crack the stone exterior of the Republican party. Through the 1990s the Republicans controlled Congress, the Supreme Court, many governorships, and state houses in America and in the next millennium they will probably continue to dominate much of American politics.

Many black leaders and elected officials do not want to hear any talk about attempting a political rapprochement with the Republicans for these reasons. It is an article of solemn faith among them that: blacks will go to their graves as Democrats; by concentrating their political strength with the Democrats they have more leverage to pry concessions out of them; and the Republicans are so deeply frozen in Christian fundamentalism, reaction, bigotry, and race baiting politics that it is hopeless for blacks to try and get anywhere with them.

There is a lot of truth on all three of these counts. There is also the gnawing reality, that for better or worse, America is a firm two party system and that will not change in the forseeable future. And since Republicans exercise so much control and power over black lives they can not simply roll over and completely vacate the field to them. This would only give the Republican power brokers and hard core race baiters an even bigger excuse to ignore or torpedo black demands. That is exactly what Reagan did in the 1980s. He ignored blacks. Blacks ignored him. And they are still paying a steep price for it. The wiser and more practical policy is to see that independent bloc voting can make or break a candidate and a campaign for both parties.

In 1960, Martin Luther King threatened to boycott both the Democratic and Republican conventions to force both parties to adopt a stronger civil rights platform. They did. In 1965, Harlem Democrat, Adam Clayton Powell having turned from preacher to politician, issued a "Black Position Paper" to the Democrats and Republicans. He called for a 20-20-20 formula when either party dealt with blacks. That meant that if blacks were 20 percent of the voters they must have 20 percent of the top political jobs, positions, and appointments. This went nowhere with the Republicans. It did with the Democrats. It marked the start of the march up the ladder within the Democratic party for black politicians.

In 1972, the Black Political Convention that met in Gary,

Indiana forced president Richard Nixon to increase minority business funding and programs. He proposed non-punitive welfare reform that was far better than what Clinton offered in 1996, and strengthen affirmative action programs especially in the trades. Again, this was far better than what Clinton offered in 1996.

In 1984 and 1988, The Jackson Rainbow Coalition pushed the Democrats to give paper support to District of Columbia statehood, national health insurance, full employment, political redistricting, and affirmative action.

In 1994, even though Republican Newt Gingrich and his bunch swept into Congress with their Contract with (some labeled it "on") America as events soon showed in the next off year election in 1998, their grip was tissue weak and in some districts they won with slightly more than 50 percent of the vote. In those same districts blacks made up a significant percent of the potential voting age population. A slight increase in the black vote would have tossed the victory to Democrats. On the other hand, the prospect of more black votes going to the Republicans would at the very least have forced them to pay some attention to black needs.

In 1996, the National African-American Leadership Summit smartly did not make the dead-end call for an independent black party or the even more dead-end and deaftist call for blacks to abstain from voting. It tried to piece together a black agenda which included the standard demands for more jobs, health care, education, and criminal justice system reform. And then called on Democrats and Republicans to endorse some, many, or all of them. That is the price that Republicans and Democrats should be required to pay for black votes.

The difficulty is that nearly all the black Democratic politicians are so comfortably nestled in the Democrat parlor few would have the daring to break ranks with them even momentarily as Jesse Jackson did in 1984 to make a real effort to get blacks to pressure the Republican and the Democratic Parties into taking their agenda seriously. Many Latino and Asian leaders and elected officials do not have those same qualms and fears. They are making huge inroads in both parties. And that is why in many places in America they are leaving blacks in the political dust.

The cruel truth is that many black elected officials are in big trouble in California and could be in greater trouble in national politics. The elected officials who adapt to the rapidly changing class and ethnic realities of states such as California will avoid the taint of corruption and scandal, and stay tuned to the needs of the poor and working class blacks. They will survive and be effective players in their state's politics. Those who can not will find themselves lost, stolen, or strayed permanently from politics and will take many blacks who look to them for leadership along with them.

VII
Remembering the *Real*
Black Panther Party

I KNEW THAT HOLLYWOOD would eventually rescue the Black Panther Party from historical oblivion. In 1995, the very short-lived movie, *Panther* momentarily dug up the Panther Party from the musty recesses of the historical dustbin. The film told a cautionary tale of what militant black leaders and organizations looked like in the 1960s and some still wistfully hope could look like again.

This revival should have been expected. Society's rebels often become the stuff of books, paintings, plays, and films. The problem is that they are either demonized or idolatrized. This happened with the Panthers. Their story is loaded with adventure and political activism, demagoguery and dedication, idealism and stupidity. I witnessed all of it during the three years the Panther star burned brightest.

In August 1967, Panther founder Huey Newton came to Los Angeles to speak. It was his first major speech outside Oakland. I talked with him afterwards. He spoke openly and enthusiastically about the Panther's programs to help the black poor. When he talked about blacks "picking up the gun" to ward off police attacks it sounded like canned rhetoric designed to get media attention and attract converts. It was not.

From the time they burst onto the national scene in 1966 with their shotguns, black berets, and tough talk; the Panthers kept the nation transfixed with a mixture of fear and fascination. The Panthers preached self-defense and anti-capitalist revolution. An amalgam of street hustlers, ex-convicts, and disenchanted student radicals, the Black Panthers were the hard men and women of the 1960s black revolution.

A month after I talked with Newton he became the first major casualty of his and the Party's rhetoric and police conflict. An early morning street confrontation in Oakland left one police officer dead and a severely wounded Newton facing the gas chamber. The Panthers became an instant symbol of the "peoples resistance" to oppression.

Meanwhile, from jail Newton directed the Panthers to organize community self-help programs that eventually included free breakfast and free clothing programs, and a voter registration campaign. Many moderate blacks and whites praised the Panthers for their efforts.

In January 1969, two Panthers were killed in a shoot-out at UCLA between the Panthers and the black nationalist US organization. The shootings at UCLA did not stop the Panthers.

Chapters were formed in more than twenty cities, and the government declared war. FBI director, J. Edgar Hoover called the Panthers "the greatest domestic threat to American security." Hoover deliberately exaggerated their numbers and importance. With the tacit support of President Nixon and Attorney General John Mitchell, he directed super-secret and illegal counter-intelligence operations against them that included: hundreds of informants, police agents, provocateurs, poison pen letters, mail covers, wire taps as well as physical threats.

• • • • • •

The tormenting cycle of police-Panther violence further enhanced their street tough reputation. This in turn brought even more raids. In December 1969, I watched the Los Angeles Police Department pour thousands of rounds into the Panther's ramshackle headquarters. The crowd cheered everytime the Panthers returned the fire. Many blacks hailed them as liberators. Yet few knew about the personal pain and suffering that these confrontations brought. I did.

I went to several funerals of slain Panthers. There were the usual fiery speeches pledging to continue the struggle. There was also the grief and tears of mothers and fathers who only vaguely understood why their son or daughter had chosen to die for the people.

I also became close friends with one of the Panther women who was arrested and convicted for her role in the Los Angeles gun battle. I spent several hours with her the day before she was scheduled to begin serving a jail sentence. She wept as I held her tightly. Yet she still firmly believed that she was fighting for a noble cause. She believed in the Panther program and had even more religious zealotry for their leadership. She was willing to suffer jail even death for them and her belief.

I talked with Newton again a few months after his conviction was reversed and he was released from jail. He still spouted the same politically correct radical slogans, but not with the same passion and sincerity as before. It appeared that he was trying to live up to the image of the defiant radical. By late 1970, the Panthers were on a permanent down hill slide. Police attacks, jailings, and self-destructive internal battles had taken a big toll. The change was evident in Newton.

In 1971, I interviewed him for a local newspaper at his Oakland penthouse apartment. He rambled and gave guarded answers to my questions. A bodyguard stood next to him the entire time we spoke. There were rumors that he and other party leaders were using and dealing drugs, had ordered Party members beaten, was extorting money from local business owners, and had siphoned off Party funds to support their elegant lifestyles. Sad to say, they were more than just rumors.

• • • • • •

Despite some of Newton's outlandish statements and destructive actions, he and Panther co-founder Bobby Seale managed to articulate a vision of change and devise specific programs such as the free breakfast and clothes programs, voter registration campaigns, free legal aid, free clinics, freedom schools, and even a failed effort to form Panther caucuses in some local labor unions. These programs had at best uneven results and were the first victims of mismanagement, outright thievery, and the Panther leaders disastrous love affair with the guns, that led to the murderous assaults by the FBI and local police. Still, they were honest efforts to empower the poor and working class blacks, and to publicly embarrass government agencies for grossly neglecting their needs of the poor.

The same honest effort could not be said to have been made by the other Panther luminary, Eldridge Cleaver. He embodied everything that a leader should not be and do. My first warning signal about this went up the first moment that I heard him speak. That was in July 1968 at a fund raising rally in Los Angeles. His speech was defiant, brash laced with profanities, and filled with threats to kill the police.

The warning flares went higher the more often I heard him speak during the next few months. His political line, if it could be called that, still had not changed. He seemed like so many of those in the 1960s and in the 1990s who called themselves radicals or even radical leaders and who make bold threats to destroy or condemn in absentia the "white establishment," "the white man," "white devil," or white oppressor."

They talk incessantly of secret plots, hidden agendas, and conspiracies against blacks. They swear that the always nebulous, unnamed white establishment is preparing the final solution to wipe out blacks. They concoct bizarre visions of detention centers, concentration camps, and Nazi-style ovens to shove blacks into. They are the same ones who refuse to join or support an organization, participate in a protest march, attend a rally, sign a petition, send a fax, letter, make a phone call to a corporation head, newspaper editor, TV station executive, or government official to protest discrimination or a specific injustice.

Cleaver, like so many persons who claim to be militants, even militant leaders, always seemed to take special delight in choosing words that had maximum shock value on crowds and minimal value in giving direction, building an organization, and developing a program that gives people tangible things they can do to make change.

He was a breed apart from Newton and Panther co-founder Bobby Seale who at least for a time tried to do this. He remained a prisoner of his tough guy image and a victim of his tough talk as other self-styled black "revolutionary" leaders. He, like so many of them, was just as inept when it came to making the transition from radical sounding mouthpiece to effective community organizer and leader. When he jumped bail and fled the country following his arrest after a shoot-out with police in 1969 his revolutionary star rose even higher with black militants, radical students and professors, and counter-culture practitioners. They finally had someone they could romanticize about and gorge themselves with hallucinations that he would bring the revolutionary Armageddon to America.

Cleaver was happy to indulge those fantasies. From safe havens in Algeria, Cuba, North Vietnam, the Soviet Union, and China, he preached death and destruction for America. Cleaver, broke, lonely, disenchanted, and with absolutely no constituency or organization (he was summarily expelled from the Panthers), finally repented, did his *mea culpas* and quietly eased back to America in the mid-1970s. The remainder of his years he floundered in political confusion, religious cultism, and crass commercialism. His personal and political legacy in death was just as confused and ambivalent in life.

When I heard of his death in 1998 and remembered ten years earlier Newton's murder in 1989, I immediately thought back to the Panther glory days. They symbolized the jumble of idealism, befuddlement, heroism, and tragedy that shadow black radical leaders and organizations. For a brief moment they inspired thousands to self sacrifice, and made an admirable attempt to aid and organize the poor only to have many of their followers drown the organization in a sea of selfishness, greed, opportunism, and nihilistic violence.

They showed that militant leaders and organizations can tap a nerve in the black communities, mobilize the black poor, fashion an agenda that deals with their needs and problems, and be effective organizers. It was fleeting but it can be done. Whenever the story of the Black Panther Party is told, this is the story that should be remembered most.

VIII
The Jesse Factor

I THOUGHT THIS REMARK by then California Governor Pete Wilson made about Jesse Jackson in 1996 was bigoted, insulting, and a political cheap shot. "Given his record, which is having the attention span of a gnat, I don't expect much follow-through." Wilson was talking about Jesse's announced recall campaign against him.

It was not surprising that Jesse had so intensely angered Wilson. At the time Wilson was the nation's most cynical, self-serving politician. He had built his reputation and name on three pillars: hatred of immigrants, pandering to law and order mania, and the demolition of affirmative action. He had craftily manipulated the state legislature and initiative process in California to destroy affirmative action.

As much as Wilson stood for everything rotten about American politics, his assessment of Jesse was true. His propensity to hit quickly on an issue, devote little or no time and attention to organizing and cultivating local leadership, snatch all the media he could, and then move on had become legendary.

Jesse's recall campaign against Wilson predictably went nowhere. It would have taken more than a million votes to qualify a recall petition for the state ballot. It would have taken months of hard work to register and mobilize voters. And no petition campaign to recall a statewide official in California had ever qualified for the ballot, let alone succeeded. Wilson like many Medieval Republican politicians who claimed that Jesse was worth thousands of white votes to them, hoped that Jesse's opposition to him would have pumped any life into his hospice bound presidential campaign in 1996. Yet the Wilson-Jesse flap was one example of the Jesse factor at work.

Another is Jesse's foreign diplomatic coups that result in the release of hostages and meetings with politically scorned heads of state. Two questions inevitably crop up when this happens. One is how can he do what presidents, heads of state, and official diplomats can not do. The second is whether what he does is good or bad for African-Americans?

● ● ● ● ● ●

The first question is easy to answer. He succeeds precisely because he is not an American or European president, head of state, or official diplomat. He has no ministerial portfolio, no legal standing, and no defined political agenda. He is an Afri-can-American activist and is not seen by the likes of Yugosla-vian strongman Slobadan Milosevic, Iraq capo Saddam Hussein, or Syria's chief Hafez Assad, all dictators that Jesse worked his magic on during the 1980s and 1990s, as an inherent enemy.

When they grant him audiences, favors, and turn over American hostages to him they can reap public relations value, put their best humanitarian face forward, make the U.S. and the Western nations look stupid, and incompetent, and gain a little face in war or foreign policy brinkmanship. During the U.S.-NATO war against Yugoslavia over Kosovo in 1999, Milosevic instantly recognized Jesse's value. In releasing three American hostages, he hoped to score a few points on the cheap with international and American public opinion.

Photo-ops at the Yugoslav president's palace and Jesse's standard trademark appeal to "give peace a chance" came dangerously close to putting a stamp of legitimacy on a barbaric regime desperate to wipe the gruesome stain of the rape, pil-lage, and murder of thousands of ethnic Albanians from its murderous hands. It also increased the U.S.-NATO's efforts to make him pay. They bombed Yugoslav cities and towns even more piteously after Jesse left the country. They were not about to tolerate the meddling of private citizen Jesse in Big Power war and foreign policy making.

Many blacks cheer loudly when Jesse pulls off his diplo-matic coups. And they should cheer. They are magnificent. No matter what the motive behind the efforts, it saves the lives of the victims and earns the eternal respect and gratitude of their families. These diplomatic conquests also enhance Jesse's image. It gives him the chance to reassert his credentials as humanitarian, religious leader, and peace advocate. It gives him the bigger chance to reassert himself as media hero, and his standing as black America's main if not only man. And this is what makes the second question whether the Jesse factor is good or bad for African-Americans harder to answer.

The reason it is so hard to answer is because there is unquestionably far reaching good policy and goodwill that results from his forays. The problem is that the good he does has been so tightly bound up with his gargantuan ego, opportunism, and worst of all the media anointing of Jesse. Some argue that all of these negatives should probably be overlooked. After all as they contend, what difference does it make why someone does something as long as something good comes out of it?

• • • • • •

It is a question that is loaded with ambivalence and doubt when it comes to Jesse. A good example of how they collide is his much touted brainchild the Rainbow Coalition which he formed in 1985. The idea was to build "a mighty coalition of conscience" as he called it with whites, Latinos, Asians, gays, and women's groups. Together they would carve out a progressive social agenda on items such as more funding for education, health care, and criminal justice system reform. Items that Republicans and Democrats routinely short-change or neglect. Their agenda would also put far less emphasis on defense and the prison-industrial complex. Items that Republicans and Democrats routinely over-emphasize. The Coalition would act as an independent political pressure group to lobby, picket, protest, demonstrate or work the margins of the political process to squeeze at least some of these things on their agenda out of the two parties.

This all sounded great for a time. Thousands of supporters signed on to the Rainbow bandwagon. They passionately believed that if anyone could pull off the challenge to the two parties Jesse could. The Coalition as Jesse saw it would be a launchpad for a candidate to harangue the Democrats to show some backbone on these issues. And who would be better to be the candidate to rally the troops than Jesse? He barged into the Democratic party state primaries in 1984 and 1988 with his Rainbow campaigns. He made good copy, became the subject of much political parlor talk, and even made a few mainstream Democratic hopefuls nervous when they saw that his campaign actually touched the nerves of more than a few voters and that included many white voters in several states.

The Rainbow Coalition's social action agenda and promise of political independence went out the window fast as soon as Jesse got a puff of influence within the Democratic party and found that he could pad his role as power broker within the party. As he moved more snugly into the inner party ranks, many Rainbow true believers cried foul that he had sold out the Rainbow Coalition's principles. However, even the most hard-line Jesse critics had to admit that his presidential bid was more than a Jesse ego show. The campaign swelled the black voter registration roles, and this made a crucial difference in putting many more black and liberal to moderate white Democrats in Congress and state legislatures during the 1990s.

One Democrat in particular owed more than a small debt of gratitude to Jesse and that was Bill Clinton in 1992 and 1996. Nearly all of those new blacks that Jesse corralled voted for him. Jesse also pretty much came off as the last liberal standing in national politics by talking up the need for more and better health care, education, support of Nelson Mandela and democracy in South Africa, opposition to Third World dictators, and more defense spending. This shamed many Democrats and a few Republicans who had scurried away from these issues as if they were the Ebola Virus

• • • • • •

The goodwill and positive benefits from the Jesse factor, however, comes with a huge cost. The cost is that it stifles local leadership and organizing efforts, and feeds into the media anointing of him as their chosen black leader. The Jesse factor began almost from the moment that James Earl Ray sent a bullet coursing through Martin Luther King's neck in Memphis in 1968. The scramble was on among black leaders and the media to crown the heir apparent to King. Jesse was a devoted and dedicated King protégé in SCLC, although far less than a personal favorite of King's.

There was much speculation among the press and civil rights leaders who would be King's replacement. Jesse was careful to join himself at the hip to King's memory. He continually reminded any and all that he believed he had been as close to King as any of King's other aides. The race for King's successor in the public and especially the media's eye was pretty much decided by *Playboy* magazine in 1969 when it made a huge presumption and declared Jesse in its interview with him, "King's heir apparent."

Jesse was determined to try and live up to the tag. During the next quarter century there was a Jesse sighting on any and every issue. His leadership modus operandi went like this: Find a hot issue such as, striking public employees, global warming, the Super Bowl, the Olympics, Rodney King, Mike Tyson, O.J. Simpson, the Los Angeles Riots, NAFTA protests, South Africa, the Middle East, Haiti, gay rights, farmworkers, or police abuse. He would blow into town, lead a demonstration or deliver a fiery speech at a rally, make vague promises to create a lasting campaign, do little or no personal organizing, and then quickly move on. The only arguable exception to Jesse's modus operandi was the battle over the expulsion of several black students from a Decatur, Illinois high school in 1999 following a fist fight at a football game. Jesse led marches and demonstrations against the Draconian punishment. He stuck with the issue much longer than usual and was justly commended for it. But this one issue, one place, one time does not mean that he has abandoned the hit and run pattern and practice of his leadership style.

And that style is still to get quick headlines and photo-ops. His reputation as leader and committed activist is preserved. The media gets its soundbite. Many whites who are hostile to black demands for political and economic empowerment get even more worked up against whatever the issue is that local activists raise. As the most visible, and seemingly outspoken, symbol of those demands, it is easy for them to transfer their antipathy to him.

When this happens local blacks and political activists get more frustrated and disillusioned when the issue they highlight or the injustice they are fighting against gets diverted into rancorous name calling and finger pointing between political activists and conservatives over Jesse's motives in championing whatever the cause is that brought him to town.

Jesse angrily bristles every time the charge that he hogs the media glare, and is incapable of any follow-through action, is hurled at him. He fires back, "I play the role of a catalyst. If I bring inspiration and direction, it is the job of the people who work there to develop the actual programs." Then with a final word that should settle the matter he compares himself to Billy Graham and insists that no one criticizes him for rolling into town with his religious big tent crusades and not staying around to minister to the converts.

This is precisely the point. Graham is not there to minister to the new converts, the local ministers do that. They and Graham understand that this is what his crusades are designed to do. He does not come to town to interfere with the work of the local churches rather, it is to boost their work. Graham has an established organization and a thriving ministry. His travel schedule is worked out years in advance to coordinate with the on-going work of local religious leaders. They know that once Graham leaves town they will not be shoved into the background and forgotten.

Jesse also forgets something else about Graham. He is a non-sectarian religious leader not a political leader. There is not the vaguest possibility of controversy or conflict in what he says or does. People do not pick and choose sides for or against him. He has one issue and one mission only and that is to spread the word of God. He does not dash off to one city after another, or one country after another chasing whatever issue strikes his immediate fancy.

If anything, Jesse presents a better contrast not to Graham but to two other fellow ministers turned politicians and much reviled activists, Pat Robertson and Louis Farrakhan. For better and worse each has a firm agenda, a solid organization, a national support network, a successful economic program, and is actively involved in local issues. Robertson and Farrakhan are national figures. They do not appear to chase the media. The media appears to chase them.

As for Jesse's jibe that he is a catalyst to give direction and inspiration, nearly all of the issues, actions, and causes that he has made an appearance on over the years, whether it is a police shooting, affirmative action, or striking workers have already sparked public outrage. Local leaders have already emerged to organize actions, frame issues and demands, inspire others to support them, and draw much media attention. If they had not, Jesse would not have been there. When Jesse leaves town the pattern instantly repeats itself. The same newspaper and TV reporters who leaped over themselves to cover the actions of local leaders initially either completely lose interest in "the story" or relegate it to the back page news. In the process they marginalize or flat-out ignore the issues they were fighting for. The oxygen has been sucked out of the issue.

••••••

This long running dance between Jesse and the media did not just happen by chance. From the moment *Playboy* anointed him as the next Martin Luther King, many in the media dutifully fell in line. It was not because they were enthralled by his captivating personality, recognized his considerable talents, or genuinely believed that he was the next King. It was because he indulged their passion to pick a black leader that they feel comfortable with. A leader that they feel has some stature and credibility, personal flair, and will not be extreme in his or her positions. The media selection of a chosen black leader is an ancient device that has been used to tap black leaders from Booker T. Washington to Martin Luther King, Jr.

The media gets away with this crass and cynical tactic because many whites regard blacks as so far outside the political and social pale of American society that they filter their view of blacks solely through the prism of race and encase them in the monolith of race. They are profoundly conditioned to believe that all blacks think and act alike. This allows them to select the chosen black leader using a criteria that is not based on whether the individual chosen has a vibrant program, strong organization, solid constituency, and superior talent.

Jesse read the tea leaves and quickly got the media's number. His compact rhymes, one liners, and clever twists of a phrase were scripted for a media which by the late 1970s was well into the first stage of replacing in-depth news with sex, sensationalism, and soundbites. He also knew that in the modern-age the media is more than the message. It has the enormous capacity to create idols, icons, and most all, celebrities. They in turn can shape and define public opinion and public policy.

Jesse was determined to make himself into that personality/idol/icon/celebrity. According to Jesse's principal biographer, Marshall Frady, he wined, dined, cajoled, cooed, fawned over, and stroked the egos of radio and TV journalists, reporters, producers, and editors. He has especially cultivated those in TV because millions of Americans are prisoners to TV celebrity star gazing and depend on it exclusively for their news, and information during the 1980s and 1990s. TV superstars such as Tom Brokaw and Dan Rather claimed that they have gotten more than one late night call from Jesse. As the consummate media networker, Jesse has made sure that there was not a reporter or TV producer breathing who did not have his name first in their rolodex when they needed a black to supply an instant quote or soundbite.

Jesse certainly can not be blamed for the angry white male backlash, racial scapegoating, or even media anointing. He is as much victim as culprit of it. Yet he cannot flee the consequence of that anointing. The media, politicians, and much of the public use the words and deeds of the chosen black leader as the standard to judge how African-Americans think and behave. When the mantle of black leadership is wrapped tightly around one man, the presumption is that he or she speaks for all blacks.

When the chosen one makes a real or contrived misstep, much of the media and the public assumes that all blacks must agree with the chosen one. They and the leader are blamed for being rash, fool-hardy, irresponsible, and prone to eternally play the race card on every social ill that befalls blacks.

In the 1980s, when Jesse first talked about forming the Rainbow Coalition, blacks were attacked as radicals. When Jesse talked about building an independent black political organization, blacks were attacked as separatists. When Jesse talked about boycotting corporations and baseball leagues that racially discriminate in hiring and promotion, blacks were attacked as disruptive. When Jesse called New York "hymietown," blacks were attacked as anti-Semitic. When Jesse talked about leading a national crusade to save affirmative action, blacks were attacked as wanting quotas and special preferences for the unqualified.

Often times blacks are forced to waste time and energy defending themselves and Jesse, or must distance themselves from him. And each time the issues get distorted or lost. He is just simply to perfect a foil for those who are hostile to those who raise issues such as police abuse, affirmative action, and increased black political empowerment to resist attacking.

Some local leaders have not figured out the Jesse factor. They still ask him to help them formulate an agenda, conduct a meeting, plan a march, hold a rally, or call a press conference. And then loudly grumble when he skips off to greener media pastures without doing any organizing work.

••••••

The debilitating cult of the leader is not Jesse's fault. He benefits mightily from it. But he did not invent it. The search for the man on the white horse to rescue individuals and groups from their pain and suffering is as old as humankind. This obsession with finding a savior is particularly endemic in individuals who are typed, scorned, and maligned as outcasts and pariahs by a dominant and powerful group within the society in which they live. They feel alienated from and powerless to take action to rid society of the forces that trap, malign, assault, and ensnare them in their pit of suffering.

Psychoanalyst Carl Jung identifies this sacrifice of self and personal identity as a flight from individuation and calls those individuals who are the recipients of the blind faith of the individual or group, "primordial images." They are collective figures such as sports heroes, celebrities, politicians, or any other popular personage whom society endows with larger than life, Olympian rank, and casts as mythical demi-gods. That individual then becomes "the leader." He is wrapped in a film of mystique and power, appears to speak the language of the people, understands their inner most needs, and possesses the messianic ability to stir their passions.

They are then free to submerge or transfer whole or a part of their identity into that of "the leader." It then becomes logical and permissible for society to depend on and root for the endowed leader to solve their problems. They believe that "the leader" can and will organize their life, provide the program, and then take the right action to implement what is in society's best interest. This absolves them of any responsibility to take charge of their lives and make or help make social change. This ability to tap into the deepest recesses of human fears and insecurities and manipulate them has been the stock in trade of demagogues, dictators, cultists, and con men since time immemorial.

The trouble is that the abandonment by individuals of responsibility to take action to change conditions in society inevitably creates martyrs, dashed hopes, and deepens cynicism. Martin Luther King and Malcolm X were the beneficiaries for a time of the mythical cloak of "the leader." Their murders left the black movement adrift and black leadership in chaos.

There is really still only one way to permanently pry loose from the Jesse factor. National and local African-American organizations, community leaders, public officials, and political activists must continue to propose pragmatic programs and strategies to combat drug and gang violence, and to promote economic and political empowerment. They must diligently work away from the glare of the TV cameras. And most importantly they must never confuse sustained leadership, consistent organization, and a coherent program with photo opportunities and press clippings.

IX
Who Is Listening To Us?

I CAN NOT BEGIN TO COUNT the times that I have heard many blacks ask, "Who is listening to us"? They are not talking about politicians, corporate executives, or government officials. They are talking about black leaders. They are talking about the issues that they feel are vital to their lives and that many black leaders ignore, distort, misinterpret, or more often than not simply self-assign themselves the job of being their voice, even though that is not always the voice with which many blacks speak with.

This cavernous breach is one of the biggest problems that traditional black organizations such as the NAACP, SCLC, and the Urban League have when they formulate their agendas. Their agenda rotates around their concerns of more affirmative action, economic parity, professional advancement, and getting more black office holders and political appointments. This is often wildly at odds with the needs of the black poor. The divide between the agenda of the black middle-class and their leaders was nakedly apparent on two of the hottest button issues that raged in the 1990s— school vouchers and the police.

••••••

The instant it appeared that Florida Governor Jeb Bush in May 1999 would bulldoze his school voucher program through the state legislature, the NAACP announced that it would file suit to stop it. The NAACP ticked off the standard arguments that vouchers are a scheme by conservatives to obliterate public education, would leave the poorest of poor students behind in even poorer and more racially isolated schools, and would perpetuate the cycle of educational neglect. Yet in a national survey the Joint Center for Political and Economic Studies, a black Washington D.C. think tank, found that a majority of black parents want vouchers. And a near whopping 90 percent of blacks between the ages of 26 to 35, who are most likely to have children attending public schools, want vouchers the most.

The wide chasm among blacks on education was a telltale sign that mainstream black leaders often march to a far different tune than poor and working class blacks. These leaders are mostly liberal, middle-class businesspersons and professionals. Their kids are safely tucked away in private schools and escape the ravages of bad public schools. Poor and working class blacks have no such luxury.

So when the mostly black Milwaukee public schools in 1990 became the first school district in the nation to authorize vouchers for private schools, the stampede by black parents to grab the money and dash their children into private or parochial schools was so great officials had to have a lottery to decide who received a voucher. To the shock of black leaders, many black activists, instead of denouncing vouchers as a right-wing threat to public schools, denounced black leaders for opposing vouchers.

The activists saw vouchers as a weapon against an insensitive, stagnant, often racist educational bureaucracy that systematically victimizes black children, and as a steppingstone toward community empowerment. The pro-voucher sentiment among many blacks was so strong that several black Congressional Democrats broke ranks with the NAACP, the Urban League, and their own Congressional Black Caucus to publicly support the Republican-backed national school voucher program.

Black parents, however, do not pluck at vouchers because of the racially and politically stacked agendas of conservative politicians and black militants. They are fed up with decaying, crime-ridden schools, terrible teachers, and indifferent administrators. They are desperate to put their children into schools that teach them how to read, write, spell, add and subtract. They want their sons and daughters to have a decent chance at a career or profession and not become prison fodder or candidates for early graves. The only thing they ask is whether vouchers will improve their children's education.

That answer is still unclear. Conservatives and black leaders trot out a handful of studies and experts to prove that vouchers are a smashing success or an abject failure. But neither side has mustered a convincing case for or against them, mostly because voucher programs are still not widespread enough in school districts nationally, and there are not enough children in the programs that do exist to tell whether they work or not. Even in Milwaukee limited funds, accessibility, and classroom space in private schools enable only a tiny percentage of the school district's low-income students to use vouchers to attend private schools. The best that the voucher combatants can do is fall back on such anecdotal homilies as "the parents love them" or "the schools are getting better."

The doomsday predictions of many black leaders that vouchers bankrupt public schools, and further squash achievement standards have so far been false fears. There was no spending plunge in public school districts where vouchers are in use and reading scores in some actually increased. Voucher supporters claim that the improvement in classroom performance can be traced to the pressure, competition, and the attention from the voucher controversy that forced teachers and administrators to do a better job in the classroom.

While the arguments of black leaders against vouchers seem sound on paper, many black parents will ignore them until public schools perform better. This means they must have more funds, better texts, equipment, teacher training programs, huge increases in cultural diversity programs, an expansion of charter and magnet schools, far greater parental involvement in decision-making on curriculum, texts, and staffing. And, most importantly, local school districts must institute an equitable system that permits them to get rid of incompetent teachers and administrators.

It also means that many black leaders must face the harsh reality that as long as many inner-city public schools disgracefully underperform, black working-class parents must have the right to pick and choose the schools that offer the best deal in education for their children. And, for now, that choice for many means vouchers no matter what their leaders think or say about them.

• • • • • •

If the idea that so many blacks could find vouchers appealing appalled many black leaders, they were almost as surprised at what many blacks said about the police. In June 1999, a Justice Department survey found that blacks in a dozen cities generally applauded the police. Many black leaders were flabbergasted at this. This flew in the face of the conventional wisdom of nearly everyone in America who read the newspapers or watched TV that blacks were inveterate cop haters. Some black leaders questioned the sample used and the racial bias of those conducting the sample. They openly challenged the motives and timing of the Justice Department in releasing the survey when they did. They claimed that it was a move to undercut the momentum of the mass movement against police violence that raged in 1999. And finally they simply denounced it as a flat out lie.

There are good reasons for their bewildered, even hostile reaction. Following the Rodney King beating in 1991 and for a good part of the O.J. Simpson trial in 1995, as well as the brutal wave of shootings of young blacks in Chicago, California, and New York in 1998 and 1999, much of the press relentlessly played up the police vs. African-American conflict. This planted the dangerous myth that the police and black communities are eternally at war. Nothing could be further from the truth. African-Americans have never been anti-police. They have been anti-racist and anti-abusive police officers.

They protest the actions of cops such as New York police officer Justin Volpe who pled guilty in May 1999 to the beating and torture of Haitian immigrant Abner Louima. They denounce the conduct of officers who engage in racial profiling of young blacks on the sidewalks, streets, and highways of America. They condemn those police officers who apply street corner justice in black communities and those police officials who whitewash their actions through the code of silence.

The small band of rogue cops who disgracefully misuse their authority make a mockery of the laws they are sworn to uphold. Most police officials and beat officers are, and should be, ashamed and embarrassed by their repulsive conduct. They realize that this only fortifies the misperception among many African-Americans that all cops are brutal. It gives many African-American leaders free rein to denounce the police. They assume that they are only expressing the wishes of all blacks. This in turn completes the farcical cycle by strengthening the conviction of the public, police, and politicians to paint all blacks as lawless and irresponsible. This gives many politicians even more ammunition to make the case for more police, prosecutors, and tougher laws.

There is another reason why many black leaders ignore or downplay the fact that most blacks have never been anti-police. Despite the mounds of news features and stories that depict young blacks as thugs, gangsters, and a perpetual menace to whites. Most whites are not at risk from black criminals. Other blacks are. They are more likely to be victims of violent crime or to have friends or relatives who have been crime victims than whites.

The same Justice Department survey found that blacks are nearly twice as likely to be victims of violence than whites. And the leading cause of death among young black males and increasingly black females under age 24 is still homicide. In nearly all cases, they will be killed by other blacks, not by the police. The overwhelming majority of those killed, injured, maimed, and victimized by other blacks, are blacks.

• • • • • •

The call by many blacks, but rarely from mainstream black leaders, for more and better police service, increased moral crusade against crime and violence, greater personal and family responsibility, more gang sweeps, injunctions, drug arrests and evictions of lawbreakers from public housing reflect their fervent desire to rid their neighborhoods of drug dealers and violent criminals. This far outweighs any supposed racial loyalties.

There have been countless defense attorneys who have fallen for the black anti-police myth and have tried to load up juries in trials of violent black criminals with as many blacks as they can. They assume that blacks are so consumed with hatred of white authority that they would nullify the law and let a black lawbreaker waltz out of court a free man or woman. They have been rudely jolted back to reality when black jurors in these cases find the evidence of guilt compelling, police testimony unbiased, and trial procedures fair. Without batting an eye, they have brought back guilty verdicts against black defendants. In some trials, they have led the charge in recommending the death penalty.

The biggest reason, however, why many black leaders and much of the public cling to the ludicrous idea that African-Americans are anti-police is that they think most blacks are poor, downtrodden, and therefore reflexively resentful of established authority. This is an even sillier myth. While the total wealth and income of blacks still pales in comparison to that of whites, the reality is that more African-Americans than ever feel that they are coming closer to realizing the American Dream. In a 1998 poll, the Joint Center for Political and Economic Studies discovered that for the first time ever more blacks than whites claimed they were better off financially than they were the year before.

This new found sense of prosperity and comfort hardly makes blacks prone to be cop-hating rebels, but rather conservative law abiding citizens every bit as anxious as whites to safeguard their property and hard earned valuables from criminals.

The saddest thing is that the phony notion that African-Americans dislike the police hardens the "us vs. them" attitude among many police officers, strengthens the deadly cycle of fear and distrust about the police, and heightens the risk of even more destructive confrontations between the police and black communities. This is far too steep a price for the public and black leaders to ask blacks to pay for the sake of perpetuating a myth.

Many blacks desperately long for school vouchers and show much more respect for police officers who do their duty fairly and protect black communities from crime and violence. Yet many black leaders turn that opinion upside down and oppose programs that many blacks want, and voice opinions that are not in line with theirs. They find themselves dancing way out of step with black communities. That is why many blacks ask: "Who is listening to us"?

X
Another Image for the NAACP

I WATCHED A PARADE of current and hopeful movie and TV celebrities flit through the aisles hugging and glad-handing each other at an NAACP Image Awards ceremony in the late 1990s. All the while they kept a close eye on the cameras filming the event for Fox-TV. Many of them were young and it seemed that the only reason they were handed an Image Awards nomination was because they appeared in a recent TV sit-com, cut a pop or rap album, or had published a kiss-and-tell biography. My suspicion was confirmed when a woman nearby muttered loudly, "Who are these people"?

Her question seemed less a question than an indictment of the event since few of the nominees had publicly said or done anything to attack racial stereotypes in the media and entertainment industry. Worse, some of these artists were guilty of promoting negative stereotypes on the screen and in their music. And some of the corporations that produced their works were even guiltier of spreading racial stereotypes and had abominable records in the hiring and promotion of African-Americans. Yet the NAACP has worked hard for thirty years to turn the Image Awards into a crowning showcase for the gliteratti of black America.

All this was a big turnabout for an event that in the early 1990s tottered on the edge of permanent extinction. The NAACP Image Awards had racked up debts that climbed to $1.5 million. This forced it to cancel the 1995 show. With the help of Northwest Airlines, Chrysler, McDonalds, donations from other corporations, and a TV deal with the Fox Network, the Image Awards was soon back in business.

The price the NAACP paid for Fox-TV and the corporations to rescue the Image Awards was to glut the event with glamour attractions. The idea was to appeal to a public hooked on celebrities and entertainers while limiting the ceremony to the mildest possible references to social activism. Meanwhile some NAACP officials turned deaf to the grumbles from many blacks that the Image Awards had become a pale imitation of the Academy Awards.

In 1997, a small group of rebels inside the NAACP found out how deaf some NAACP officials had become. They denounced the Image Awards for nominations of awards to stars of TV sitcoms who are among the worst image assassins of blacks. NAACP officials responded with a terse reprimand of Warner Bros. for showing its "contempt" for African-Americans by its grotesquely racially stereotyped and clownish portrayal of them on the *Warner Brothers TV Network* and then quickly moved on.

I had to do a hard search through the distant recesses of my memory to remember how the NAACP had practically put itself on the political map back in 1915 when it waged a titanic battle against the most lurid racist film ever made in America, D.W. Griffith's *The Birth of a Nation*. The battle was to protect the black image from the sport of vile humor, ridicule, and insult that Griffith's film unabashedly took great historic license in doing. NAACP officials shadowed the film from city to city, and set up picket lines, demonstrations, boycotts, and legal suits to try to stop it cold in its tracks. And everytime over the next few decades when someone would try to sneak a showing of it somewhere the NAACP would be right there with their attorneys and demonstrators.

Even less well known but in some ways more significant, NAACP officials toyed with the idea of financing their own film to tell the true story of the black experience. The lack of money stopped them. But if they had pulled this off it would have set a strong model and example for generations to come of how blacks do not need to rely on Hollywood to tell its story. They can make their films and tell that story themselves.

I also remembered that up to and through World War II, NAACP officials jealously guarded the black image every chance they got. They raised the same howl of outrage and threatened to employ the same protest tactics in the early 1950s against the slapstick buffoonery of the *Amos 'n Andy* show. They complained that the show butchered the black image. The series lasted one year and was yanked from the air.

• • • • • •

The Image Awards plummet into celebrity showcasing and hob knobbing with a frenzied pursuit after corporate dollars underscored the monumental retreat by NAACP officials from visible cutting edge social activism. That retreat can be directly traced to the collapse of legal segregation in the 1960s, the class divisions that imploded within black America, and the greening of the black middle-class. This was a process that has been slowly evolving since the murders of King and Malcolm X in the 1960s. The civil rights organizations and black power groups were victims of the success and failure of movements they sparked and inspired.

By the close of the 1960s, these movements had spent themselves. The torrent of demonstrations, sit-ins, marches, and civil rights legislation annihilated the legal wall of segregation. The obstructionist red-neck, Southern politicians, nightriders, police dogs, and murderous sheriffs vanished from public view. They were the hard symbols of white oppression.

They were that era's most dependable strawmen. Civil rights leaders could always point to and use them to rally all blacks, rich or poor, against racial injustice. The black power leaders fared even worse. Their appeals for black consciousness, black pride, the study of African history, and culture, made it respectable, almost obligatory, for blacks to shout "I'm black and I'm proud." That was more than enough for many blacks.

With King and Malcolm gone from the scene, and no leader with the power, depth, and moral authority they possessed to take their place, black organizations crumbled into a stupor of infighting, personal clashes, jealousies, and paralysis. The federal government was more than eager to try and finish off the remnants of black militancy. The FBI through its vast arsenal of illegal weapons that included wiretaps, surveillance, harassment, jailings, physical assaults, and a small army of provocateurs waged a vicious war against the civil rights and black power movements throughout the 1960s.

It crowned its war with victory when it effectively knocked into permanent oblivion the Student Non-Violent Coordinating Committee, the Panthers, for a long period SCLC, and the Nation of Islam. Many of their most sincere, dedicated, and politically active members were intimidated, frightened, and discouraged. They gave up and drifted away from these organizations and the insight, dedication, and zeal they had for taking leadership in community struggles died or drifted away with them.

During the 1970s and 1980s, there were economic shocks to the American economy that also hurt the poor and black workers. They included: galloping inflation, OPEC price shocks, plant closures, corporate restructuring, mergers, downsizings, the rise of Pacific Rim nations and Mexico, as banking and manufacturing power houses, and the deterioration in much of public education. These shocks smashed many of the social and economic gains made by black workers in the 1960s. The Reagan-Bush administrations pulverized job, education, and social programs that aided the black poor and women. Sociologists and the media rechristened the black poor with the tag of the black underclass.

While there was bad news for one segment of black America, there was good news for another. The black middle-class was having a field day. They were starting more and better businesses, marching into more corporations and universities, spreading out into more of the professions, winning more political offices, buying bigger and more expensive homes, taking more luxury vacations, and joining more country clubs than ever before in the history of America.

This split between two black Americas one poorer and more desperate, and the other more prosperous and complacent was mirrored in the leadership style and programs of mainstream black organizations. The NAACP, Urban League, and SCLC were now in a hot chase for more Small Business Administration loans for minority businesses, partnerships, pacts, and convenants with corporations, more advertising dollars for black-owned radio stations, and more corporate deposits in black-owned banks.

Mainstream black leaders also made a core part of their agenda the hunt for more: scholarships and grants for middle-income students to prestigious universities; more corporate managerial positions and corporate board of directors appointments; more school busing; more elected officials; and more state and local Republican and Democratic party appointments. These became the buzzwords heard from the 1970s into the 1990s, none of which had even the remotest bearing on the lives of the black poor.

There was certainly nothing inherently wrong with their venturing after the promised and long denied American dream.

They were merely following the well-worn path tread by earlier European immigrants and the more recent immigrants from Asia and Latin America. Many of them also trekked out of their slums, ghettos, barrios, borscht belts, Little Italy's, Chinatowns, and Little Tokyos into thriving businesses, professional careers, and political offices.

The difference between their odyssey in America and that of blacks was that the European ethnics had to overcome the barriers of language and poverty but not racial oppression. The non-white immigrants had to overcome the same barriers, plus the added plague of racial discrimination, but not the legacy of slavery. This legacy has always weighed the heaviest on the black poor. This guaranteed that when blacks made a quantum leap in social and economic gains in the 1970s, the gains would be confined primarily to those deemed the best and brightest among blacks, i.e. the black middle-class, and not the black poor.

While blacks had been the loyalist of foot soldiers for the Democrats since the 1930s, in the 1960s they had finally gotten their reward for their fierce loyalty with a few Great Society social programs, civil rights, and voting rights laws. At the same time, the black poor were getting even more hopelessly lost in the shuffle in the American economy and society. They could not turn to their traditional benefactors, the Democrats, for help.

Desperate to get back in the White House after the cold-shoulder of the Reagan years during the 1980s, party leaders led by Clinton's "New Democrats" were hellbent on recapturing the millions of middle-class and blue collar whites fed up with what they perceived as the Democrats tilt toward blacks, minorities, women, and the poor. They had jumped the Democratic party ship *en masse* in the 1980s. Clinton got many of them back by out Reaganing Reagan. He promised to cut or purge welfare and social programs, downsize government, hire more police and prosecutors, build more prisons, and pass more punitive laws. And he did.

••••••

The men and women who called the shots in the NAACP, still the nation's oldest and premier protest and advocacy organization, were trapped in the middle by the twisting political trends and shifting fortunes upward of the black middle-class and downward of the black poor. Their bind was even more vexing since many of them had ground their teeth on the civil rights battles of the 1960s and knew first-hand the disastrous toll that poverty and political disenfranchisement had on many blacks. And there were many NAACP officials in some local chapters determined to resist the lure of prosperity, comfort, and inertia. They continued to be visible activists on the issues of police brutality, job and housing discrimination, media racism, and labor exploitation in the 1990s.

NAACP president Kweisi Mfume seemed to understand the bind of his organization. He candidly admitted that the NAACP faced dangerous times and was at a critical point in its history. He fingered the usual villains the hard line Christian fundamentalists, National Rifle Association, militias, anti-abortionist groups, the borderline racist Council of Conservative Citizens, race baiting politicians, right-wing private think tanks, and the legion of assorted hate mongering crackpots. Faced with these formidable and deadly foes, Mfume called for more activist leaders in the struggle.

Even as Mfume warned of the dangers and appealed for new leaders to meet the present and future challenges of the new Millennium, he and NAACP officers still broke into cold sweats over the memories of the NAACP's disastrous plunge into financial pauperism in the 1980s. They were resolute that that must never happen again. This depended on two things.

First, they would have to intensify their efforts to win greater concessions from corporations for more jobs and promotions for the black middle-class. Second, they would have to try to turn the spigot up even higher on the dollars they received from corporations. To attain both goals, it demanded that they stay in the good graces of corporate America and no longer rely for their main support on the nickels and dimes of the poor and working class blacks who had financially floated the organization through the first half century of its existence into the 1960s. By the 1990s, the shift was plainly evident. The NAACP's official publication, the *Crisis* magazine was stuffed with corporate ads and constant pitches for sponsors for the NAACP's fundraising campaigns, dinners, banquets, scholarship funds, and programs.

The shift toward greater corporate accommodation was also evident the few times that NAACP leaders hit the picket lines or staged a demonstration. They demanded such things as more clerks on the Supreme Court, more fair share hiring pacts with hotels and restaurants, more managers and executive promotions in corporations, and more diversity in the TV industry business loans and training programs. These were solid, doable, but safe goals.

The NAACP did not entirely abandon grittier issues such as police abuse. After the ghastly shootings of Amadou Diallo in New York in February 1999, and Tyisha Miller in Riverside, California in December 1998, Mfume called on Clinton and the Justice Department to monitor and withhold funds from police departments that refuse to crack down on the officers within their departments who repeatedly resort to deadly force. The NAACP officials were pretty much forced to take this action. The wave of shootings had triggered a firestorm of outrage among blacks reminiscent of the protests in 1991 following the acquittal of the four LAPD officers that beat Rodney King.

• • • • • •

Even with these welcome displays of visible activism, NAACP officials have still largely been publicly missing in action on these pivotal issues in the 1990s:

•The billboards, TV, and radio ads by companies that targeted young blacks with alcohol and tobacco ads.

•The catastrophic health hazard that toxic dumps, waste sites, and landfills located in/or near black and low income neighborhoods pose to many poor and working class blacks.

• The spread of repressive and regressive Three Strikes Laws in many states. These laws lock up mostly poor black and Latinos for what amount to life sentences for mostly non-violent offenses.

• The dreary plight of thousands of black children trapped in an oftimes poorly funded and negligent foster care system in many states.

• The horrific escalation of black women in prisons and the heart rending condition of their children left behind.

• The refusal of Congress to amend the disparity in the mandatory sentencing laws on drug use and sale. This disparity in the laws has done much to skyrocket the numbers of blacks in state and federal prisons.

The NAACP billed its thirtieth annual Image Awards ceremony in 1999 as a salute to "50 years of entertainment and 90 years of courage." Its only hope of living up to this billing in the early years of the new Millennium is to aggressively attack the pulsating issues that confront poor and working class blacks, refuse to take money from those corporations that promote unequal opportunity, and initiate the renaissance of visible activist leadership to take its place on the frontier of social change. Until then the image of the NAACP will be that it promotes entertainment but not courage.

XI
The Unselling of Malcolm X

I REMEMBER THAT EXHILARATING moment in 1992 when Malcolm X was not only the talk of the town but the craze of the nation. I saw a middle-aged Latino male parking cars and sporting a cap emblazoned with the letter "X." I saw a white teenager standing at a street corner bus stop with an "X" T-shirt. I saw a nattily dressed black accountant at a business meeting wearing a Kente scarf with a large "X" in the middle. That same week there was a full page ad in the *Los Angeles Times* that featured young men and women modeling "X" imprinted T-shirts, sweatshirts, scarves, and hats. The products carried stiff price tags and were sold in major department stores.

Fashion retailers were not the only ones cashing in on the Malcolm X craze. Book publishers went into absolute delirium for those few months. They rushed everything they could squeeze between two covers that constructed, reconstructed, deconstructed, unconstructed, and re-re-constructed Malcolm and sprinted to the bookstore shelves with them.

Since Malcolm was now a bonafide celebrity, it was only fitting that the celebs get in on the action. Madonna sang about him. Supreme Court Justice Clarence Thomas and then Vice President Dan Quayle said he influenced them. President Clinton sported an "X" cap. Even conservative mouthpiece, Rush Limbaugh, thought there was something positive about Malcolm's philosophy of black self-help.

Much of the public and the press breathlessly counted the days until the release of Spike Lee's film on Malcolm X. The film would supposedly complete the transformation of Malcolm from the much maligned in life as a racial fanatic and long forgotten in death to an all-American pop idol. The flip-flop in turning a leader inside out and defrocking his significance could be likened to the former Communist regimes practice of rehabilitating former leaders that had fallen from grace long after they were safely resting in a far removed grave and memories of them were deemed politically harmless.

Movie critics proclaimed Lee's *Malcolm X* a happening. It was not. Many of the critics panned it as: Too long, too boring, too self-serving, too watered down, or too distorted. The under age 30 crowd stayed away in droves, and it quickly died at the box office. Those that did see and enjoy the film left theaters thinking that they knew all they needed to know about him.

The flood of new books on Malcolm X immediately began to gather dust on bookstore shelves, clothing retailers changed fashion lines, and black filmmakers for the next few years found big profit and Hollywood acceptance in pumping out a morally defective and socially bankrupt parade of sex romps, goof ball comedies, and boys in the hood "gangsta" glorification flicks rather than socially-themed films.

● ● ● ● ● ●

This was not the first time that Malcolm had been harshly dumped back into the netherworld of forgotten heroes. In the years following his assassination in 1965, black militants revered Malcolm X, but the general public forgot him. Bookstore shelves groaned with biographies of Martin Luther King Jr., W.E.B. DuBois, Paul Robeson, Adam Clayton Powell, Roy Wilkins, Whitney Young, and many lesser known black figures.

Cities named streets, parks and buildings after black politicians, personalities, and historical figures. The media ran countless features on black issues. Apart from a few bootleg records of Malcolm's speeches, a collection of his speeches by a radical publisher, and a gossipy, hatchet job biography, the only full length testament to his life was his own autobiography.

Then something happened in the late 1980s. Young blacks who were not born when Malcolm lived discovered him. They listened to rap groups such as Public Enemy weave his speeches into their lyrics. He sounded tough, brash, defiant, and faintly outlandish. They loved it. They had suddenly found a hero.

With a hawk eye alertness to the twists and turns of American cultural trends, Hollywood and Madison Avenue spotted a fad in the making. They sniffed dollars. Malcolm meet the MTV, rap, Hip Hop generation. Why not, he was heaven sent. A lot had changed in the quarter century between Malcolm's murder in 1965 and Lee's film, *Malcolm X*. The Vietnam war was a distant memory. The campuses were quiet. The once rebellious inner cities, it appeared, had sunk into a hopeless morass of self-inflicted drugs and violence.

The civil rights leaders of another generation were dead, retired, or comfortably lodged in corporations, universities, public and private think tanks, government agencies, or political offices. The Soviet Union had folded up shop. America had taken on the softest of soft targets in Panama, Grenada, and Iraq and won! The search for enemies was over. The cynicism and retreat to know-nothingism of the Reagan-Bush years of the 1980s had triumphed as Americans stifled a yawn over the great moral issues of the past such as racism, poverty, and inequality.

Students chased MBAs. Communities screamed for more police and prisons. Politicians sought refuge in old fashioned "family values" and Americans gorged themselves on their new passions for VCRs, cell phones, Windows any year computer models, the Internet, and CD-Roms. Ideology was not only at an end, it had become a dirty word. And since things in America are always twisted into commodities, why not turn ideology into a commodity too. Malcolm's turn had come again.

Even with the monumental shift to social and political know and do-nothingism in America, Malcolm still would not have been even a momentary happening if young blacks had not been so desperate for leadership that they felt they had to reach back a quarter century and snatch a dead man from the grave and make him their leader.

The economic and social crisis of the 1980s and the early 1990s slammed young blacks hard. One out of three was in prison, on parole, or probation. Their unemployment and school drop-out rates soared, the right wing assault on job and social programs intensified, black youth employment remained, despite the happy-days-are-here-again-times of the 1990s, still stubbornly locked into double digit figures. They were subject to racial profiling, and "Driving While Black" vicious stops and harassment by the police. They were abandoned by mainstream black leaders who failed to provide them with credible role models, economic, and social supports, or a sense of racial pride and awareness.

The onslaught of these social ills rudely bumped many black youth to the far outer fringe of society. Many seethed at their social abandonment by many black leaders, and were jaded by the smug hypocrisy of some. They saw many black politicians, church leaders, and community leaders themselves eternally panting after sex, cash, and material comforts.

Many found in the words of Malcolm X the solution to their frustration and discontent. It was a phenomenal find for them. Malcolm was not just a fiery leader who cursed out the "white devil" and advocated black pride, economic self-sufficiency, independent political action, militant struggle, anti-militarism, third world solidarity, and women's and human rights. The problem with this was that young blacks are the offspring of the MTV-Hip-Hop Generation. They were seduced by the repackaging and myth making of Malcolm. They bought the product, tinsel and all, rather than the man.

They ignored, or never even knew, that Malcolm studied. He wrote. He debated. His own life was one of change, growth and personal inspiration. He founded an organization, the Organization of African-American Unity, and devised a far-reaching, practical program for economic self-help and political empowerment.

They did not understand that his revolt and by extension his brand of leadership was as much against the rampant materialism of America as it was against its stifling treatment of African-Americans. He would have been repelled by the self-indulgent grab for expensive cars, clothes and cash by blacks, young and old, and, especially, by many of those who called themselves black leaders.

The 1960s forerunners of today's rappers, the Last Poets, probably got it right when they said that blacks loved to hear Malcolm rap but they did not love Malcolm. That was certainly true of many black leaders in the 1960s and probably just as true in the 1990s. His message was too harsh, raw, and truth-laden. It trampled on their leadership ground. When all is said and done, Malcolm was never designed to be a mass market commodity. He was a leader who was not for sale, unlike many others who are called leaders.

XII
The Elixir of Wealth

I WAS FASCINATED WATCHING many black leaders in the 1990s gallop to promote wealth as the elixir to cure the social pains of blacks. They claimed that it would work its wonders when blacks get more businesses, start and join more investment clubs, encourage more entrepreneurs, buy more computers, and grab more corporate positions. In other words, get rich, richer, and even richer still. The irony is that when Booker T. Washington said pretty much the same thing at the turn of the 20th Century, militant black leaders led by the NAACP's W.E.B. DuBois roundly savaged him.

The debate over whether blacks should pursue what was then simply called self-help vs. militant activism raged for more than a decade. Washington's backers, mainly black businessmen, farmers, ministers, and Republican politicians, swore that racial salvation could come if blacks worked hard, saved their money, prayed regularly, stayed sober, and always remained on the look-out for any and every opportunity to get rich. Washington's challengers who were mostly upwardly mobile, Northern college educated professionals minced no words and blasted this line as at best political defeatism, and at worst a plunge back into quasi-slavery.

As the NAACP grew in strength and the civil rights movement gathered steam, Washington's program was discredited as outdated and reactionary. During the 1960s, Washington's name became an epithet young black militants flung at anyone whom they considered an "Uncle Tom."

Few among the 1990s elixir of wealth crusaders would dare resurrect Booker T. Washington as their hero. However, they have three perfectly good reasons for resurrecting his approach and making it the centerpiece of the black agenda.

Reason one. The massive cuts in job programs and social services coupled with the assault on affirmative action and civil rights during the Reagan era in the 1980s, left black leaders frustrated and dismayed with government. The conviction grew among black leaders that the government had become an enemy rather than an ally of the black poor.

Reason two. There is the much talked about anywhere from an estimated $150 billion dollar to a wild side estimate of $600 billion dollar black economy. Whatever the true figure, the money is spent yearly on goods and services. Black leaders believe that these dollars can be recycled into thriving businesses and community programs that can provide jobs and social services for the black poor. Black economic strength, black leaders say, will ultimately translate into greater political power for blacks.

Reason three. Black leaders point to the phenomenal economic success of the Jews in the first half of the 20th Century, as well as the Korean, Chinese, Vietnamese, and Cuban immigrants in the second half of that century. They have prospered in business, finance, real estate, manufacturing, and retail trade. They have built powerful business and trade associations that provide capital, credit, and technical training for their members. Equally important, their political influence in Miami, New York, Los Angeles, San Francisco, and other cities has grown with their economic clout.

••••••

At first glance, these seem to be powerful reasons why the elixir of wealth presents the best antidote for black ills. It requires taking another glance. The Jewish experience first. It was and is totally different from that of African-Americans. Many Jewish consumers know that many Jewish merchants have a socially ingrained sense of responsibility and duty to give back to their communities. This economic bonding is the product of centuries of religious and social persecution suffered in the ghettos of Russia and Eastern Europe. Jewish consumers know that at least a portion of the dollars they spend with Jewish merchants will be funneled into a wide array of social, cultural, and community programs and services from which all Jews benefit.

There is some similarity between the racial experiences in America of blacks, Asians, and Latinos, but only some. Despite much vicious discrimination, violence, color barriers in some states and locales, and decades of racist exclusion acts aimed at preventing Asians from entering the United States, non-white immigrants were still viewed as immigrants. Blacks were chattel slaves. This difference is crucial and must be constantly restated whenever the temptation arises to contrast the progress of non-white immigrants with the supposed malaise of many African-Americans.

During slavery the planters maintained iron control over their black chattel through military and political force, economic domination. The slave system systematically shattered family ties and fostered rivalries and divisions. It twisted science and religion to construct a powerful mythology of black inferiority. Emancipation did not heal the profound and painful scars of slavery. The massive campaign of terror and violence by the former planters during the Reconstruction era in the South stripped blacks of political rights and reduced them to economic outcasts.

The legacy of slavery was the scarlet letter that stamped many blacks with the unalterable stigma of inferiority. This hideously skewed and disfigured relations between blacks and whites. More hideously, this legacy poisoned the attitudes of many non-white immigrants toward blacks almost from the first moment that they touched down on American soil.

I have chosen the Vietnamese, Cubans, and Korean immigrants as examples to contrast their experience with blacks for four reasons. They are the most recent immigrants. Many escaped from countries torn by war or revolution. The majority came to the U.S. during or after the major civil rights battles of the 1960s broke down the barriers of legal segregation and sheared off the hardest edges of racial discrimination for blacks and non-white immigrants. They are for the most part non-whites.

The Vietnamese. Despite the devastation and trauma of fleeing a war-ravage country and Communist rule, the first wave of Vietnamese refugees were not impoverished, unskilled, and uneducated. The majority were high school graduates. One out of three was a college graduate. One out of three was a professional. In most cases, they arrived in America with their families intact. Many of them were wealthy property owners and merchants in Vietnam. They opened restaurants, retail stores, and hotels in their expanding community. Their Little Saigons in various cities soon became neither little or looked anything like the Saigon from which they escaped.

The second wave of Vietnamese immigrants that hit the country in the 1980s were poorer, less educated, and skilled. They were immediately eligible for counseling, job training, and public aid programs.

As refugees from Communism, nearly all of the Vietnamese, no matter when they came to America, directly benefited from a comprehensive and costly resettlement program the likes of which had never before been made available to immigrant groups in the United States.

The Cubans. The first wave of Cuban refugees who came to

America in the early 1960s were hardly dirt poor campesinos. Many were wealthy landowners. Seven out of ten had worked in the professions, trades, or operated businesses. Four out of ten were college educated. Eight out of ten had earned more, and in many cases far more, than the average income of other workers in their homeland. The federal government and many state governments paid their resettlement costs, provided welfare and income subsidies, and loans and grants to Cuban business persons. Far from being a model of bootstrap uplift, the immigrants were helped every step along the way by the generosity of the government and lending agencies.

Despite media attention and public panic over the criminals and misfits that arrived in the second and third wave of Cuban refugees in the 1980s, they also received generous housing and relocation subsidies from the federal government and state governments.

The Koreans. The love-hate relationship that many blacks have with Korean immigrants was graphically and tragically demonstrated in the tempest of violence in Los Angeles in 1992 following the acquittal of the four LAPD officers who beat Rodney King. Black rioters took their revenge out on Korean-owned stores. They claimed that the Korean merchants were rude, discourteous, sold shoddy goods, and charged extortion prices for their products. Even while many blacks vilified Koreans and burned their stores, they proclaimed them the ideal model to emulate if blacks were to build wealth. It is not that simple.

During the 1920s, Korean newspapers called America a

boon to the Korean immigrants and noted that Koreans were very grateful for the opportunity to prosper. That same decade more than 200 African-Americans (at least by official count) were lynched in America. By the close of the 1920s, Koreans in the United States were still only a small fraction of the population of blacks. However, Korean businesspersons had opened hundreds of barbershops, laundries, retail and grocery stores, and a national hotel chain. They were not viewed by the leaders of lily-white unions and white politicians as labor threats. They suffered discrimination, but they were not dumped in broken down Jim Crow schools or barred from owning property in many white neighborhoods.

In the 1970s, the second big wave of Korean immigrants arrived in this country. The vast majority had professional or technical training. And a sizable number had either owned or managed property and businesses in Korea. They had strong and cohesive family and cultural ties, and belonged to well-organized trade organizations. Most belonged to a Korean cultural or ethnic association. The Korean government gave many of them a nice send off to America when it permitted them to take up to $100,000 from the country to start new businesses.

There were no specific government programs to aid the Korean immigrants as there were with the Vietnamese and the Cubans who were considered war refugees. With their business backgrounds and association connections, many Koreans found the doors of the financial industry open to them. In Atlanta, in the 1970s, when blacks were barely able to get a cup of coffee at a restaurant or a room at a downtown hotel, a majority of Korean business owners in the city were able to secure loans or credit from the city's banks.

In the 1980s, the ranks of Korean immigrants in the United States swelled. Korean businesspersons transformed many blocks in Los Angeles and other cities into industrial and commercial showpieces complete with resplendent office buildings and commercial shopping malls.

Black leaders point to the success of Europeans and non-white immigrants and preach to blacks that this is the path they can take to solve many of their problems. However, they should also point out that their path was not strewn with the same obstacles as that of blacks.

• • • • • •

While many blacks do not enjoy the instant entree to business and government resources that the immigrants received, black leaders who hail the elixir of wealth insist that they can still stockpile the billions of consumer dollars blacks spend into a formidable power base. The problem is that black consumer dollars are just that — consumer dollars.

Despite their impressive increase in the number of blacks in managerial, technical, and professional positions in corporations, the overwhelming majority of the 12 million or so black workers in America are still concentrated in clerical, services, and the trades. A sizable proportion of blacks are employed as unskilled laborers. The black median income has stubbornly held at slightly more than half of the white median income.

When it comes to net wealth, the gap between blacks and whites is even more appalling. The average for white households is about ten times more than that of blacks and that gap has not budged an inch even with the prosperity of the 1990s.

The budget cuts during the Reagan-Bush-Clinton years pushed more blacks into the ranks of the unemployed. Even in the prosperous years of the 1990s, about one out of four blacks still remained nestled permanently below the poverty line. Many of them lacked competitive technical and labor skills, and became even more marginalized and unemployable. For many, crime became their only means of survival.

The chronic poverty and income disparity has always meant that blacks have very little discretionary income or savings. Their paychecks are spent almost exclusively on basic household goods and services. The major corporations exercise near monopoly domination over their consumer dollars since they control production, supply, and transport of all basic food and household items.

This is no accident. The economic infrastructure of African-American communities historically has never been designed for capital retention or inflow. The unbending control of domestic markets by major corporations is akin to a kind of domestic colonialism. Black consumers buy their goods almost exclusively from white producers. In turn, the black workers serve as a low-wage pool of labor for them. Capital flight from black communities deliberately keeps black business at the outer border of the corporate economy.

A look at the economy of the ghetto today still shows that the traditional business patterns have changed little. The small mom and pop, catering, beauty and barber shops, and small grocery stores still make up the bulk of old or start-up businesses in African-American communities. They are almost always sole proprietorships capable of providing employment only for the owner or his/her family members. They are straitjacketed by the problems of small business--higher prices, limited stocks, and a narrow consumer base. The bulk of these business owners face the same dilemma that all small businesses face, little capital, business expertise, and a high failure rate. On top of that, they face the even bigger dilemma of being black, poor, and discriminated against.

The piles of black magazines and newspapers are crammed with get rich quick articles, features, and success stories. They show spiffily dressed, beaming *nouveau riche* young blacks. The articles hail their entrepreneurial successes in petroleum and energy, manufacturing, automotive sales, investment, equity trading, and communications. They do not tell readers that their companies did not provide large-scale employment for the blacks and have a large failure rate. These are largely finance and capital intensive industries that create few jobs. They provided employment for much less than one percent of the general black work force.

That is because the top black firms are subject to the same market fluctuations as white corporations. If inflation-conscious consumers buy fewer cars, new clothes, radios or tapes, auto dealers, clothing manufacturers, and electronic assembly firms are hurt—no matter what the color of the owner.

Black-owned Savings & Loans are a good case in point. They directly felt the shock waves from the S&L shakeout in the 1980s. One out of three black S&Ls nationally could not meet the minimum tangible capital requirements established by government regulators. And one out of five was declared insolvent and placed under direct government supervision.

While some black firms have prospered, many prospective black entrepreneurs still find the door pad locked when they seek credit and capital from lending agencies or managerial and technical training from corporations. The result is that black capitalism is still largely an unrealized dream. The several billions in annual sales the *Black Enterprise 100* racked up in the 1990s paled beside the trillions of dollars in sales by *Fortune* 500 companies. The total sales for all of the *BE* top companies together was less than that of one of the mid-list *Fortune 500* companies. Overall, gross revenues for black business still hovers at a small fractional percent of the corporate total. The relative strength of black business vis-à-vis the American economy did not change even during the 1990s get-rich-quick years for black business growth.

Some eventually pulled out of their nose-dive, expanded, and prospered. Other new black firms blossomed during the 1990s. They became positive examples of black entrepreneurial resilience, that inspired young budding black professionals and businesspersons to try their hand in the business world and even provide minimal employment and business opportunities for blacks.

They encourage blacks to form more black business councils,

associations, and chambers of commerce. The moderate success of some black businesses has also encouraged some black activists to revive the decades-old idea of establishing black united funds to provide loans, grants, and other forms of assistance to local community improvement groups. These are all positive and much needed efforts that deserve the support of blacks, especially black businesses and professionals.

In return for this support, black leaders and businesspersons must do some heavy soul searching and ask themselves: What are the limits of race loyalty? They are asking black consumers to forgo convenience and savings to loyally support black businesses soley because they are black. Yet they are not saying what black businesses are willing to give in return. They have presented no visible blueprint that shows how black dollars in their hands will be used to provide concrete economic and social benefits.

●●●●●●

These efforts alone can not solve the gigantic social and economic difficulties of poor and working-class blacks. Black leaders and organizations can spearhead that effort by organizing community task forces to confront the problems of poverty, lack of quality education, and poor neighborhood services, organizing more political action groups to increase black voting strength and initiating mass protest drives to put perpetual pressure on local and national elected officials and business leaders to deal with these problems and issues. State and federal governments should be challenged to provide more aid and assistance to revitalize African-American communities.

With the Soviet Union out of business, the world relatively peaceful, and the unprecedented boom in the 1990s economy, there is absolutely no economic excuse why the state and federal governments could not provide more low interest home loans, encourage small business expansion, fund a national health insurance plan, rebuild the crumbling infrastructure of the inner cities, and support art and cultural projects. This would create thousands of private and public sector jobs for African-Americans.

The money is there, and will be there for some years to come. In 1999, government and private economists projected a $1 trillion surplus in the federal budget through the year 2015. Even if this figure is on the high side, and is only the talk of self-serving politicians, the stability in the U.S. and world economy pretty much guarantee that the massive federal deficits of past years are a thing of the foreseeable past anyway.

Black leaders are certainly not wrong when they insist that blacks can and should do much more to help themselves. For them, however, to prescribe the acquisition of wealth as the principal, or worse, the only elixir for the social ailments of the poor and working-class blacks is an insufficient potion.

Conclusion
The Reappearance of Black Leadership

I HAVE HEARD THESE QUESTIONS asked almost as often as the question "Where are our leaders"? The questions are, "Who is a leader"? "What is a leader"? "Do we really need leaders"?

The answer to these questions can not be answered until blacks exorcise the romantic whimsy that sprouted in the post 1960s civil rights meltdown, and was helped generously along by the O.J. Simpson, Princess Diana, Monica Lewinsky gossip, smut, and crime mongering media of the 1990s. That whimsy was that any blacks who had a boisterous voice, TV camera magnetism, and could get whites infuriated at them was a leader. Many blacks confused media popularity with leadership or even relevance.

There are two vital ingredients that go into real leadership. The first is that a leader is made, not born. The tag of leadership can be claimed by anyone who is positive and productive in whatever they do, makes a solid contribution to the enrichment of their community, and influences others to do the same. They show by their example that they are willing to tackle community and social problems. This could be anyone—a parent, tradesperson, professional, businessperson, artist, or a scholar—anyone.

The important thing is that individuals working alone if need be, but preferably with other concerned individuals, and even more preferably within an organization must be prepared to identify needs and problems. They must also frame the issues in such a way as to attract support, build public consensus for action, develop a coherent strategy for change, and not jump ship or panic if, but more likely when, established political leaders or name organizations do not lift a finger to help.

The second ingredient is that leaders do not need a mass following to be effective. They need an issue that evokes public outrage, and the strong belief that action needs to be taken. The idea that change can not be made unless thousands are in the streets marching for a cause is another romantic whimsy from the 1960s. In the postscript, I detail how I and a handful of people made significant change in the case of the shooting of Margaret Laverne Mitchell, a homeless African-American woman by a Los Angeles Police officer in May 1999.

●●●●●●

Yet I understand why many blacks ask those questions. They are in a headlong search to find a way out of their crisis. They are tired of propping up celebrities and sports icons as leaders and role models. They know that when they fall from grace, much of America, and that includes many blacks too, swiftly and brutally turn on them.

They are forced to ask these puzzling and perplexing questions because the murders of Martin Luther King and Malcolm X, the destruction of the Black Panther Party, and the splintering apart of the Nation of Islam in the 1960s was the turning point for the black movement. Without a leader to command the respect of the black poor and even middle-class blacks and a cohesive program to unite them, the black movement plunged into a disastrous sink-hole. As we move into the next Millennium it still has not dug itself out of that hole. This has caused cataclysmic headaches for traditional civil rights organizations which have prevented them from fully mobilizing African-Americans around crushing problems within local communities.

• • • • • •

The void left by traditional black leaders and organizations on cutting edge social issues has been filled nationally and in many cities by community activists, concerned residents, and some local ministers. They have formed coalitions, ad-hoc groups, committees and associations to battle the major problems of Driving While Black, racial profiling, police misconduct, redlining, lending and corporate discrimination, HIV/AIDS affliction, the infuriating disparities in the criminal justice system, drug and alcohol addiction, three strikes laws, the soaring incarceration rates of black men and women, deteriorating public schools, access to affordable health care, and the especially brutal plight of poor, black women.

They have stepped up to provide solid leadership on issues such as advertising for alcohol and tobacco products, the proliferation of liquor stores, toxic waste sites, sexual violence, the repulsive depictions by Hollywood and much of the media of poor blacks, the lack of education, and improved neighborhood services. Here are some concrete examples of how leaders step forward that are not generally thought of as leaders.

Many young blacks have organized stop the violence marches and rallies in several cities. They have made more blacks not only aware of the disproportionately high levels of violence within some black communities but also the physical abuse of African-American children in many black homes. They are leaders, too.

Many dedicated black social workers, psychologists and health professionals nationally have begun programs to mediate, and counsel parents in anti-violence prevention techniques, and train African-American volunteer "child advocates" in child counseling. They are leaders, too.

Many chapters and individual members of the 100 Black Men organization nationally sponsor mentoring programs and provide scholarships and grants to young blacks. There has been a series of "black male crisis" conferences nationally in the 1990s in which black professionals and businesspersons shared their experiences with hundreds of high school and junior high school students. They are leaders, too.

Many black educators, businesspersons, and professionals periodically sponsor conferences in which they provide parents with learning tips and materials to help them improve the study habits of their children. Their efforts also point to the even greater need for black professionals and educators to create self-help programs that provide educational scholarships, career counseling, and job and skills training programs to break the mesmerizing Air Jordan sports effect and recycle those young blacks who are sports junkies into serious students. They are leaders, too.

Many black parents are active in PTAs, teacher-parent councils, school volunteer associations; and hold teachers, school administrators, and board of education officials accountable for the quality of their children's education. They are leaders, too.

Many black elected officials and ministers rejected the inertia, ignorance, and downright hostility of many black ministers and leaders and formed a consortium in 1999 to battle the HIV/AIDS crisis. A number of religious groups took the lead in the fight against the dread disease. They are leaders, too.

In cities throughout America there are dozens of coalitions, community councils, rites of passage, and mentoring groups that have sprung up in black communities to deal with local problems. Although these groups have widely divergent objectives, they have four things in common.

They are not dependent on the traditional civil rights organizations or black politicians for political and financial backing. They were created in direct response to local problems and the lack of established leaders and organizations to confront these issues. They do not depend on the personality of a media anointed leader. They use a montage of tactics such as boycotts, demonstrations. They write, send faxes, mail, telephone calls, with pressure campaigns to the press, politicians, city officials, corporate leaders. They rally and use political lobbying that is a near textbook throwback to the 1960s type and style of activism.

• • • • • •

The most frightening quandary facing black leaders is that of poor and working-class black women. They are under massive assault from drugs, sexual violence, police abuse, poverty, and imprisonment. They have gotten little or no support from mainstream black organizations and women's groups to take up their cause. The Million Woman March was a valiant, but not wholly satisfactory attempt to correct that leadership travesty. With almost no media attention, few high profile participants, and fewer still endorsements from established black leaders, they pulled off a magnificent fete when they brought nearly one million women to Philadelphia in 1997. Their drive and determination must be saluted.

Ultimately they suffered the same problems as did the Million Man March. A few women went back home and worked hard to build their local committees into real action groups. In some cities, they sponsored voter registration drives, business development programs, workshops on domestic violence, and campaigns on police abuse. Their efforts were short-lived. The women of the Million Woman March were long on energy and short on follow-up plans and programs to fulfill the promise that brought them to Philadelphia in the first place. Yet the Million Woman March, as the Million Man March, stands as a useful model for future local community organizing.

• • • • • •

National and local community activists and organizations by taking initiative and action on issues vital to black communities have changed the concept of who is a leader and what constitutes a program for action and social change.

They do not reduce leadership to media grandstanding photo-ops, or soundbites, or celebrity status. They do not draw corporate sponsors. They will not win popularity contests. They do not grab a spot on national TV talk shows such as *Oprah, Nightline, Meet the Press*, or *Face the Nation*. They will not become household names and their contributions will be recognized by only a handful. They will guarantee the reappearance of effective black leadership.

Postscript

Blueprint for Seizing Leadership Anatomy of the Justice for Margaret Mitchell Campaign

I WAS AT A RESTAURANT when I read the first account of the shooting of Margaret Laverne Mitchell in May 1999. The story was sketchy. It said only that an unnamed homeless woman, stopped for questioning about an alleged pilfered shopping cart from a local supermarket, was shot and killed by a Los Angeles police officer when she lunged at him with a screw driver. The story sounded too pat. My warning antenna inched up immediately. I wondered: Who was this woman? What had she done to bring about the confrontation? Why were police stopping someone with a shopping cart when you can drive down any street and see people pushing carts? I also wondered if this was the same, smallish, frail-looking black woman that I had seen on several occasions sitting alone or curled up on a bus stop bench near downtown Los Angeles?

Just at the moment I tossed these nagging questions from my mind, a local community activist, excitedly drove up and asked if I heard the news about the shooting. I said "yes." I told him that I knew nothing about it other than what was in the newspaper. He quickly answered my questions. Yes, she was homeless. Yes, the police had stopped her because of her shopping cart. And, yes, she was black.

But there were holes in the police version of the shooting. He said that he had talked to two employees at a nearby car dealership who witnessed the shooting. Both disputed the police version. They swore that Mitchell did not pose a threat to the officers and was shot as she walked away. We felt that a police investigation would likely clear the officers of any wrongdoing. It did.

I remembered Attorney General Janet Reno's much publicized promise to black leaders in March 1999 that the Justice Department would vigorously monitor police abuse cases and prosecute more officers accused of excessive force. We decided to call a press conference the next day at the site of the shooting to question the police version of the shooting. At the press conference, we were joined by several other community activists. We called for a full investigation by the Justice Department and the Los Angeles Police Commission to determine if the officers used excessive force in the Mitchell shooting.

The next day we got what we asked for. The Assistant U.S. Attorney, announced that the Justice Department would probe the shooting. Los Angeles Mayor Richard Riordan also called on the Police Commission to conduct a complete investigation.

The Commission promised to take a hard look at the shooting. This was a start. But we were not satisfied. We immediately formed the Justice for Margaret Mitchell Coalition to plan future actions around the case.

We felt that the Mitchell shooting provided a rare window of opportunity to discuss the problems of the lack of treatment services for needy mentally ill persons, homelessness, race and gender discrimination, and police abuse. We reached out to homeless rights advocates and mental health professionals to hold joint protest actions. We held a demonstration and rally the same week at the Los Angeles Police Department's central headquarters against police abuse and a press conference at a neighborhood shelter and alcohol and drug treatment center to spotlight the lack of funds and treatment programs for homeless persons who suffer mental disorders and are dumped on the streets.

Following the press conference, coalition members and homeless rights advocates met with the U.S. Attorney in Los Angeles. We left the meeting with a firm pledge that the Justice Department would conduct a full investigation, provide progress reports on the investigation, and refer the case to the Justice Department's criminal division for possible prosecution if they found the officers used excessive force and the Los Angeles Police Department took no action. The big question was what would the LAPD do? We watched closely for a sign. As it turned out, we did not have long to wait.

● ● ● ● ● ●

The reaction to our protest actions was swift and furious from LAPD Chief Bernard Parks. In monumentally ill-advised and ill-tempered shoot-from-the-lip remarks, Parks blasted the protesters for playing the race card. This is exactly what we did not do. From the start, we made it clear that we regarded the Mitchell slaying as an issue of social and economic justice.

In our press conferences, tributes, and protest actions we never charged that Mitchell was gunned down because she was black. We blamed her death on the disgraceful failure of the system to provide adequate funding and more programs for the care, treatment, and shelter of the homeless, as well as for those who suffer mental disorders. We chided the public for treating the homeless as America's untouchables and viewing them with a disastrous mix of contempt, shame, and embarrassment.

We used the Mitchell slaying to ask these questions: Why was she on the street in the first place? Where are the treatment centers for the thousands of men and women like her? Why have not local and state officials done everything in their power to get more funds for the care of people such as Mitchell? When will state legislators reverse the horrific policies of the Reagan years that closed scores of treatment centers and offered mental health care to only those deemed violent?

This policy dumped thousands of men and women such as Mitchell on the streets. What is the policy of the LAPD toward the homeless and those with mental disorders that roam city streets? These were our prime concerns and we felt those should also be the concerns of those who profess to care about the issues of economic and social justice.

We also deliberately not did not use the Mitchell shooting to make a grand indictment of the police for the rash of shootings and acts of misconduct nationally. We kept the spotlight exclusively on the dismal situation of the thousands of homeless victims such as Mitchell. We wanted to insure that we had broad consensus from the public and the media that the Mitchell shooting was an outrage that could not be ignored. We also wanted to enlist the support of homeless rights advocates and mental health professionals in our campaign.

To energize the public on these issues, the coalition held a spirited Justice for Margaret Mitchell Walk from the neighborhood supermarket where we suspected that Mitchell and other homeless persons in the area got their shopping carts to the site at where Mitchell was gunned down. The walk was part tribute, part testimonial, and part challenge to city officials to enact badly needed reforms in law and public policy toward the homeless and those with mental disorders who are forced to fend for themselves on the streets.

We were not entirely able to overcome the deep complacency and indifference of much of the public to the difficulties of other people such as Mitchell. That especially included nearly all the city's black politicians, ministers, business and professional groups. In short, the city's traditional black leadership establishment. Even without them we notched these triumphs:

•A firm commitment from the Justice Department to fully investigate the shooting.

•A statement from the Mayor of Los Angeles that the city is sincerely attempting to grapple with the problems of the homeless.

- A challenge by some Los Angeles City Council members to the LAPD's tactics and procedures in dealing with the homeless and those with mental disorders on the streets.
- A pledge by some legislators to re-examine funding and treatment programs for the homeless and the needy who suffer mental disorders.
- A new found awareness among many persons toward the ills of the homeless and those with mental disorders on our streets. The coalition members tried to do everything possible to make sure that Margaret Laverne Mitchell got the justice in death that she did not get from this society in life.

• • • • • •

In the days after the Mitchell shooting, I talked with many black community leaders and activists in Chicago, New York, Cincinnati, Dallas, Houston, and a few other cities. They had heard about the campaign for justice for Mitchell. They wanted to know how we had harnessed public outrage and gained support within the community and among city and federal officials to get the results that we did without little support from black leaders. I sensed the frustration underneath their anxious questions.

They also had major problems not only with police abuse, but also with housing, job discrimination, and crumbling public schools in their cities. They were even more frustrated at the abysmal failure of local black organizations, elected officials, and many black ministers to speak out on their concerns.

I went over and over with them how we overcame the apathy and indifference of black leadership in Los Angeles in the Mitchell case and waged a solid campaign for justice. It took time, patience, dedication, and most importantly a belief by us that an injustice had been committed that screamed for redress. This was our blueprint for seizing the reins of leadership. I believe this example could be a blueprint for others as well.

Bibliography

Robert L. Allen, *Black Awakening in Capitalist America* (New York:Doubleday, 1969).

Ball, Howard, *A Defiant Life: Thurgood Marshall and the Persistence of Racism in America* (New York: Crown Publishers, 1998).

Barbour, Floyd B., (ed.), *The Black Power Revolt* (Boston:Porter Sergeant, 1968).

Barone, Michael, *Our Country* (New York:The Free Press, 1990).

Black Scholar, (ed.), *Court of Appeal: The Black Community Speaks Out on the Racial and Sexual Politics of Thomas vs. Hill* (New York:Ballantine Books, 1992).

Boyte, Harry C., *The Backyard Revolution: Understanding the New Citizen Movement* (Philadelphia:Temple University Press, 1980).

Branch, Taylor, *Parting the Waters: America in the King Years, 1954-1963* (New York:Simon and Schuster, 1988).

—*Pillar of Fire: America in the King Years, 1963-1965* (New York:Simon and Schuster, 1998).

Carson, Clayborne, *The Eyes on the Prize Civil Rights Reader* (New York:Penguin, 1991).

Clay, William L., *Just Permanent Interests* (New York:Amistad Press, 1993).

Frady, Marshall, *Jesse: The Life and Pilgrimage of Jesse Jackson* (New York:Random House, 1996).

Franklin, John Hope, *From Slavery to Freedom* (New York:Random House, 1969).

Frederickson, George M., *The Black Image in the White Mind, 1817-1914* (New York:Harper & Row, 1971).

Glasgow, Douglass G., *The Black Underclass* (New York: Vintage Books, 1980).

Guinier, Lani, *The Tyranny of the Majority: Fundamental Fairness in Representative Democracy* (New York:The Free Press, 1994).

Haley, Alex and Malcolm X, *The Autobiography of Malcolm X* (New York:Ballantine, 1965).

King Jr., Martin Luther, *Where Do We Go From Here: Chaos or Community?* (New York:Harper & Row, 1967).

Oliver, Melvin and Shapiro, Thomas M., *Black Wealth, White Wealth: A New Perspective on Racial Inequality* (New York:Routledge, 1997).

Lee Martin A. and Solomon, Norman, *Unreliable Sources: A Guide to Detecting Bias in News Media* (New York:Lyle Stuart, 1991).

Lerner, Gerda, (ed.), *Black Women in White America* (New York:Pantheon, 1972).

Lerner Eric K. and Holmes, Mary Ellen, *AIDS Crisis in America*, second edition (Santa Barbara, Cal.:ABC-CLIO Inc., 1998).

National Urban League, *State of Black America, 1995* (New York:Urban League,1995).

—*State of Black America, 1996*
—*State of Black America, 1997*
—*State of Black America, 1998*
—*State of Black America, 1999*

Nelson, Hart, *et.al.*, *The Black Church in America* (New York:Basic Books, 1971).

Preston, Michael B., *et.al.* (ed.), *The New Black Politics* (New York:Longman, 1982).

Seale, Bobby, *Seize the Time* (New York:Random House, 1970).

Silberman, Charles, *A Certain People: American Jews and Their Lives Today* (New York:Harcourt Brace, 1976).

Steele, James B., *America: What Went Wrong* (Kansas City:Andrew & McTeel, 1992).

Takaki, Ronald, *Strangers From a Different Shore: A History of Asian Americans* (New York:Penguin, 1989).

Zangrando, Robert L., *The NAACP Crusade Against Lynching, 1909-1950* (Philadelphia:Temple University Press, 1980).

Reference Notes

Introduction

I devoted several of my syndicated newspaper columns to the many aspects of the Sherrice Iverson tragedy in 1997 and 1998, the campaign to get child protective legislation, and the prosecution of David Cash for his involvement in the Iverson death. These columns appeared in the *Los Angeles Watts Times* and dozens of other black newspapers nationally in August and September 1998.

Volumes have been written on the black power and civil rights movements of the 1960s. Two of the more comprehensive are Clayborne Carson, *The Eyes on the Prize Civil Rights Reader* (New York: Penguin, 1991). Carson, SNCC, and the *Black Awakening of the 1960s* (Cambridge:Mass: Harvard University Press, 1995). Two other works that I found indispensable in understanding the politics and activism of the 1960s are Robert L. Allen, *Black Awakening in Capitalist America* (New York: Doubleday, 1969) and Floyd B. Barbour (ed.), *The Black Power Revolt* (Boston: Porter Sargeant, 1968).

Chapter I
The Shameful Silence of Too Many Black Ministers

Few subjects have sparked more passion and controversy among blacks than the role of the black minister and the black church. Nearly everyone has an opinion on what they should and not do. My concern is what they should do more of. Martin Luther King, Jr. blisters black ministers who refuse to be leaders in the battle for the spiritual AND social renewal of blacks in *Strength to Love* (New York:Harper & Row, 1963) and *Stride Toward Freedom* (New York:Harper&Row, 1958).

The books I found most useful in detailing the general strengths and weaknesses of the black church are, E. Franklin Frazier, *The Negro Church in America* (New York:Schocken Books, 1969). Gayraud S. Wilmore, *Black Religion and Black Radicalism* (New York:Anchor Books, 1973) and Hart Nelson, *et.al.* (ed.), *The Black Church in America* (New York: Basic Books, 1971).

Apart from King, Adam Clayton Powell, Sr. and Jr., still stand out as the best examples in the 20th Century of activist, politically involved black churchmen. Charles V. Hamilton admirably captures their life and work in *Adam Clayton Powell, Jr.* (New York:Atheneum, 1991). The tidbit about the NAACP's reliance on black ministers in the early years is in Howard Ball's, *A Defiant Life* (New York:Crown Publishers, 1998).

Taylor Branch gives a blow-by-blow account of the raucous conflict between King and Jackson that briefly tore apart the National Baptist Convention in *Parting the Waters*, and *Pillar of Fire* (New York:Simon and Schuster, 1988 and New York: Simon and Schuster, 1998). The greed, corruption, and pursuit of power that became the trademark of the era of president Ronald Reagan is detailed in Robert Lekachman *Greed is Not Enough* (New York:Pantheon Books, 1982). The issues of police violence and the corruption trial of Reverend

Henry Lyons were covered extensively in the *Los Angeles Times, Washington Post,* and *New York Times,* and on the National Baptist Convention's website www.nbcusa.org.

The shattering ruin the HIV / AIDS crisis wreaks on black communities is presented in stark detail in Eric K. Lerner and Mary Ellen Hombs (eds.) *AIDS Crisis in America,* second edition (Santa Barbara, Cal.:ABC-CLIO Inc., 1998), 152-154. Ronald J. Weatherford in *Somebody's Knocking at Your Door: AIDS and the African-American Church* (New York: Haworth Press, 1998) takes sharp issue with black churchmen for their anemic response to that crisis by many black churchmen during the 1990s.

The human rights group, Amnesty International, does the best job of documenting police misconduct in America. Its website is www.amnesty.org The biblical references are from *The King James Bible* (Collins World).

Chapter II
The Dilemma of Two Kings

A sketchy view of where the Southern Christian Leadership Conference under Martin Luther King III is heading can be found on its website www.sclc.org. The life and work of Dr. Martin Luther King, Jr. has been dissected and pieced together so many times and in so many ways in books, magazines, and speeches it practically defies count. But the absolute best books on him are David Garrow, *Bearing the Cross* (New York: William Morrow, 1986), Taylor Branch, *Parting the Waters: America in The King Years, 1954-1963* (New York: Simon and Schuster, 1988), and *Pillar of Fire: America in the King Years, 1963-1965* (New York: Simon and Schuster, 1998).

James M. Washington has put together an excellent compilation of King's writings and speeches in *A Testament of Hope* (New York: Harper & Collins, 1986) In his hard-hitting work, *Where Do We Go from Here: Chaos or Community?* (New York: Harper & Row, 1967), King offers his own pragmatic vision of change for America.

Ward Connerly and conservative Republicans pathetically misued King's fragmented words on what later came to be called affirmative action in the debate over the anti-affirmative action ballot initiative proposition 209 in California in 1996. Their shameless tactics were detailed in articles in the *Los Angeles Times* during 1996.

Chapter III
Whither the Congressional Black Caucus?

William L. Clay gives a good insider's view and defense of the history and workings of the Congressional Black Caucus in *Just Permanent Interests* (New York: Amistad Press, 1993). More inside material about the CBC's policy initiatives can be found on the CBC's website www.cbc.org and the website of former CBC chair Maxine Waters www.house.gov/waters. For a far more critical view of the CBC, see Marguerite Ross Barnett, "The Congressional Black Caucus: Illusions and Realities of Power," in Michael B. Preston, (ed.), *et.al.*, *The New Black Politics* (New York: Longman, 1982).

The *Los Angeles Times*, *Washington Post* and *New York Times* are important sources for specific events, activities, and policy initiatives of the CBC during the Clinton years. Also Joe Feagin and Melvin P. Sikes detail the monumental damage racial stereotypes have caused African-Americans in *Living With Racism* (Boston:Beacon Press, 1994).

My criticisms of Clinton's views on affirmative action, crime, and racial stereotypes were taken directly from speeches and addresses in various articles in the *Los Angeles Times* and the *Washington Post* from 1995-1998.

Chapter IV
The Tattered Tale of Two Icons

As of 1999 there were no full blown biographies of Bill Cosby or Ron Brown. I relied on a variety of articles in the *New York Times, Los Angeles Times*, the *Washington Post*, and *Christian Science Monitor* for background on the legal and political travails of both men and their careers.

Camille Cosby's honest remarks blaming American racism for the murder of her son Ennis appeared in an article in *USA Today*, July 10, 1998. A sample of the hysterical reactions by the circus of talk show hosts, and their listeners, see the comments of David Horowitz. They can be found on the website of Larry Elder, www.larryelder.com Elder is a talk show host on KABC radio in Los Angeles.

Chapter V
Why Speak for Black Women

The lack of attention paid by mainstream black organizations to the devastating crisis of black women in prison is mirrored in the lack of attention paid to it in the black press. The rare exceptions are *Emerge* and *Essence* magazines which ran a couple of articles on specific prison cases involving women in 1997 and 1998, and a column by Bernice Powell Jackson, the *Civil Rights Journal* (May, 17, 1999). The Prison Activist Resource Center presents the most comprehensive assessment of the conditions and treatment of women in America's prisons. Its website is www.prisonactivist.org.

The murderous assaults on black women at Rosewood, Florida in 1921 and in the years from 1900-1930s are detailed in Michael D'Orso, *Like Judgment Day* (New York: Putnam, 1996) and Robert Zangrando,

The NAACP Crusade Against Lynching, 1909-1950 (Philadelphia: Temple University Press, 1980). The sordid saga of myths, and lies, and the brutal social and economic exploitation of black women is detailed in an expanding number of books by black women writers. I found these most useful, Gerda Lerner, *Black Women in White America*, (ed.), (New York: Pantheon, 1972); bell hooks, *Talking Back, Thinking Feminist, Thinking Black* (Boston: South End Press, 1989), and Black Scholar, (ed.), *Court of Appeal: The Black Community Speaks Out on the Racial and Sexual Politics of Thomas vs. Hill* (New York: Ballantine Books, 1992).

Donald Boggle deals with the image assassination of black women in *Toms, Coons, Mulattos. Mammies and Bucks* (New York: Continuum Publishing Co., 1989). The U.S. Census reports and the Urban League's annual State of Black America reports for 1996, 1997, 1998, 1999 provide a wealth of useful stats and information on the plight of poor black women.

Nearly every edition of *Essence, Upscale*, and *Todays Black Woman* showcases the success of black professional and business women and their near obsession with relationships, fitness, hair, and fashions.

The Million Woman March in 1997 got nowhere near the publicity and did not stir the same high volume of discussion, controversy, and media interest as the Million Man March did in 1995. The *Christian Science Monitor, New York Times*, and *Washington Post* did day after stories on the event and then said not another word about it. Details on the event and the organizing efforts around it can be found on the website of the *Philadelphia Tribune*, www.phila-tribune.com/related-mwm.htm. NAACP president Kweisi Mfume's position on the March can be found on the NAACP's website www.naacp.org.

Chapter VI
Black Politicians: Lost, Stolen, Strayed

The legal and political chess match that spanned much of 1998 between Donald C. Smaltz, the independent special counsel who prosecuted Agricultural Secretary Mike Espy, is detailed on his website www.oic.gov The criminal case against Espy was extensively covered in the *Washington Post, Los Angeles Times*, and the *New York Times*. I relied on the same newspapers for accounts of the sex, drug and corruption trials of Marion Barry, Walter Tucker, and Mel Reynolds. Helen A. Cooper in "A Question of Justice: Do Prosecutors Target Minority Politicians," in the *Wall Street Journal*, January 12, 1996, raised the strong possibility that black politicians were being targeted for harassment and prosecution by the Reagan administration.

The *Los Angeles Times* and the *Oakland Tribune* were the main sources on the state assembly election fiasco of Elihu Harris in February,1999, and the Jerry Brown mayoral race in November 1998. The U.S. Census reports are the best source to see how far blacks have sunk and Latinos have risen in politics and in population numbers. Its website is www.census.gov.

Despite the astronomical leap in the number of black elected officials in America since the 1970s there is a surprising shortage of books on the subject of black politics in the 1990s. The best I found on black political fortunes and misfortunes and the attempts by blacks during the past century to bolt from the two parties and go it alone politically are Lucious Barker and Jesse McCrory, *Blacks in the American Political System* (New York: Winthrop, 1980); Hanes Walton, Jr. *Black Political Parties* (New York:Free Press, 1972); and Michael B. Preston, *et.al.,The New Black Politics* (New York:Longman, 1982). In September and October 1996, *The Final Call,* was the only newspaper to pay serious attention to the National African-American leadership Summit and its convention.

Chapter VII
Remembering the *Real* Black Panther Party

Panther co-founder Bobby Seale still provides the best first hand account of the Panthers rise in *Seize the Time* (New York:Random House, 1970). Eldridge Cleaver's *Soul on Ice* (New York:Dell, 1992) is a mostly self-serving rationale for his criminal life. He sheds almost no light on his motives for getting involved with the Panthers. Even though Hugh Pearson's *The Shadow of the Panther* (New York:Perseus, 1995) got much right about the Panthers, it still comes off as a gossipy, hatchet job of a book.

Philip S. Foner did a solid and invaluable job of collecting the speeches, writings, and internal materials from Panther leaders that appeared in the *Black Panther Newspaper* weekly from 1968-1970, in the *Black Panthers Speak* (New York:J.B. Lippincott, 1970).

The absolute best view of the war of annihilation waged by the FBI against the Panthers and black radicals in the 1960s is Kenneth O'Reilly's, *Racial Matters: The FBI's Secret File on Black America 1960-1972* (New York:Free Press, 1989). My assessment of the good, the bad, the ugly about the Panthers is drawn from my personal memories of, and experiences with them during their brief heyday from 1967 through 1969.

Chapter VIII
The Jesse Factor

The exploits of Jesse Jackson as politician, activist, and statesman; his conflicts with politicians such as California Governor Pete Wilson; and his triumph in Kosovo in 1999 were well-documented in numerous newspapers and magazine articles in the 1980s and 1990s. I have relied on them for background information on Jesse and my assessment of his doings. The program, philosophy, and achievements of his organization PUSH and the Rainbow Coalition can be found on the Rainbow/PUSH website www.rainbowpush.org.

There are a string of books that have tried to make sense out of what Jesse is about. The three most important are Marshall Frady, *Jesse: The Life and Pilgrimage of Jesse Jackson* (New York: Random House, 1996) Adolph L. Reed, Jr., *The Jesse Jackson Phenomenon* (New Haven:Yale University Press, 1986) and Karen L. Standford, *Beyond the Boundaries: Reverend Jesse Jackson and International Affairs* (Albany: SUNY Press, 1997).

King's true right hand man was Ralph David Abernathy. He details the ambiguous relationship Jackson had with King and the other SCLC leaders in *And The Walls Came Tumbling Down* (New York:Harper & Row, 1989). The awsome power and dominance of the major media to make and break people and issues, shape public opinion, and distort the news has been well-documented by Ben Bagdikian, *The Media Monopoly* (Boston:Beacon Press, 1990), James Aronson, *Packaging the News* (New York: International Publishers, 1971), and Martin A. Lee and Norman Solomon, Unreliable Sources: A Guide to Detecting Bias in News Media (New York:Lyle Stuart, 1991). Also any edition of the media watchdog group Fairness and Accuracy in Reporting's monthly publication *Extra!* contains a storehouse of exposés on media dominance and bias.

The three social, psychological, and religious studies of the cult of the leader I relied on were John D. Goldhammer, *Under the Influence* (Amherst, NY: Prometheus Books, 1996); Carl Jung, *Researches into the Phenomenology of the Self* (Princeton, N.J.:Princeton University Press, 1969); and Eric Hoffer, *The True Believer: Thoughts on the Nature of Mass Movements* (New York:Harper & Row, 1951).

Chapter IX
Who Is Listening To Us?

Nearly every argument in favor of school vouchers can be found on the web site of the conservative educational think tank, School Choices, www.schoolchoices.org. Nearly every argument against school vouchers can be found in the monthly newsletter, "Culture Watch," December 1998. The NAACP lays out its position against vouchers on its web site www.naacp.org The Justice Department survey in 1999 on black attitudes toward the police can be found on the Justice Department's web site www.usdoj.gov.

For an analysis of the reasons behind the epidemic of black against black crime and violence see William Oliver, "Sexual Conquest and Patterns of Black-on-Black Violence: A Statistical Cultural Perspective," Violence and Victims #4 (1989), 260-280. Ellis Cose gives a solid overview of the greening of the black middle-class and also the survey from the Joint Center for Political and Economic Studies in "The Good News About Black America," *Newsweek*, June 10, 1999.

Chapter X
Another Image of the NAACP

There is still no comprehensive history of the NAACP's magnificent pioneering triumphs in breaking the back of legal segregation and democratizing America for all Americans. But there are many books that tell fragments of the story, I used Howard Ball's biography of Thurgood Marshall, *A Defiant Life*, Roy Wilkins, *Standing Fast: The Autobiography of Roy Wilkins* (New York:Viking, 1972), and Walter White, *A Man Called White* (New York:Viking, 1948), and Robert L. Zangrando, *The NAACP Crusade Against Lynching, 1909-1950* (Philadelphia:Temple University Press, 1980).

A better picture of specific programs and initiatives, the shift toward more corporate reliance, and the political and economic fiasco the NAACP Image Awards found itself in can be found in its house organ, the *Crisis*, and on its web site www. naacp.org.

Three useful books that tell of the unraveling of America from the 1960s-1980s are Michael Barone, *Our Country: The Shaping of America from Roosevelt to Reagan* (New York:The Free Press, 1990); Donald L. Bartlett and James B. Steele, *America: What Went Wrong* (Kansas City:Andrew & McTeel, 1992), and Joel Kurtzman, *The Decline and Crash of the American Economy* (New York:W.W. Norton, 1988).

Clinton and the so-called New Democrats strategy to Out Reagan Reagan and take back the White House from the Republicans in 1992 is detailed in Christopher Hitchens, *No One Left to Lie To* (New York:Verso, 1999).There is little or no mention of the tormenting issues of tobacco and liquor industry advertising that targets young blacks, black women in prison, the three strikes laws, Hollywood and TV industry racism, environmental racism, and other cutting edge issues in the *Crisis*, in NAACP press releases, or on its web site www.naacp.org.

Chapter XI
The Unselling of Malcolm X

There were numerous articles in the *New York Times, Los Angeles Times, Washington Post*, and various black newspapers in October and November 1992 that capture the feel of the momentary mania around Spike Lee's film, *Malcolm X*. The three best books on the life and times of Malcolm and the Nation of Islam, are Alex Haley and Malcolm X, *The Autobiography of Malcolm X* (New York:Ballantine, 1965), Claude Andrew Clegg III, *An Original Man, The Life and Times of Elijah*

Muhammad (New York:St. Martins, 1997). Michael Friedly, *Malcolm X: The Assassination* (New York:Carroll & Graff, 1992). Malcolm's speeches are in *By Any Means Necessary* (New York:Merit Books, 1970), Bruce Perry (ed.), *Malcolm X: The Last Speeches* (New York:Pathfinder, 1989).

Douglass G. Glasgow, *The Black Underclass* (New York:Vintage Books, 1980) and Alphonso Pinkney, *The Myth of Black Progress* (New York:Cambridge University, 1989) detailed the massive social and economic mugging of black youth in the 1970s and 1980s.

Chapter XII
The Elixir of Wealth

For an excellent perspective on the titanic debate waged between the backers of Booker T. Washington and W.E.B. DuBois over political activism versus economic accommodation as the best path to black freedom at the turn of the 20th Century see August Meier, *Negro Thought in America, 1880-1915* (Ann Arbor, Mich.:University of Michigan Press, 1968) and Louis Harlan, *Booker T. Washington: The Wizard of Tuskeege, 1901-1915* (New York:Oxford University Press, 1983).

There are volumes of books that tell the story of the Jews rise in America. The two I relied on were Charles Silberman, *A Certain People: American Jews and Their Lives Today* (New York:Summit Books, 1985) and Irving Howe, *World of Our Fathers: The Journey of the East Europeans to America and the Life That They Found and Made* (New York:Harcourt Brace, 1976).

The number of books, articles, and studies on Cuban, Vietnamese, and Korean immigrants in America is growing. The sources I found most useful were Ronald Takaki, *Strangers From a Different Shore: A History of Asian Americans* (New York:Penguin, 1989); Pyon Gap Min, "Problems of Korean Immigrant Entrepreneurs" in Fred Pincus and

Howard J. Ehrlich, *Race and Ethnic Conflict* (New York:Westview Press, 1994) 253-263; and Daryl Harris, "Generating racial and Ethnic Conflict in Miami:Impact of American Foreign Policy and Domestic in James Jennings (ed.), *Blacks, Latinos, and Asians in Urban America* (Westport, Ct:Praeger, 1994) 79-94. Their are several good essays on black, Asian and Latino conflict cooperation in Ismael Reed (ed.), *MultiAmerica* (New York:Viking, 1997).

The two finest works on slavery and the enduring disfiguring of the black image in the American mind are John Hope Franklin, *From Slavery to Freedom* (New York:Random House, 1969) and George M. Frederickson, *The Black Image in the White Mind, 1817-1914* (New York: Harper & Row, 1971).

The good and the bad economic and social news for black America can be found in Ellis Cose, "The Good News for Black America." *Newsweek*, June 10, 1999 and Alphoso Pinkney, *The Myth of Black Progress* (New York:Cambridge University Press, 1989). No matter whether one thinks it is the best or worst of worlds for blacks there are many blacks that are still gripped in a vise of poverty and neglect.

The books that detail the colonial-like status and near permanent economic separation of poor black neighborhoods from mainstream America are Manning Marable, *How Capitalism Underdeveloped Black America* (Boston:South End Press, 1985), James Boggs, *Racism and the Class Struggle* (New York:Monthly Review Press, 1970), Andrew Hacker, *Two Nations* (New York:Scribners, 1992), and Melvin Oliver and Thomas M. Shapiro, *Black Wealth, White Wealth: A New Perspective on Racial Inequality* (New York:Routledge, 1997).

Black Enterprise magazine does a solid job of chronicling where black business is and where it should be. Derek Dingle takes a concise look at the problems and prospects of black business in "Whatever Happened to Black Capitalism," *Black Enterprise*, August 1990, 160-168. Black business and professional success stories are standard fare in any issue of *Ebony, Essence, Upscale* and *Black Enterprise* magazines.

Michael Barone details the impact of the federal government on improving black economic and social fortunes in *Our Country* (New York:The Free Press, 1990). The unabashed use by corporations, defense contractors, banks, and savings and loans of the federal government as their own personal piggy bank has been well-documented by the public watchdog group Common Cause, and Donald L. Bartlett and James B. Steele in *America: What Went Wrong?* (Kansas City:Andrews & McTeele, 1992).

Index

A

African-American Community,
    economic infrastructure, 144
Affirmative Action, 46-47, 81
Anti-Police, 109-113

B

Barry, Marion, 74

Black Business, 142-144

Black Churches,
    ministers, 13-28
    social justice, 14-18
    civil rights, 18-19
    police abuse, 22-23
    HIV/AIDS, 23-24

Black Family Crisis, 34, 120

Black Leaders, 1-5, 11-12, 105-
113,
    school vouchers, 106-108
    public schools, 109
    police and black community,
    109-113

characteristics of, 147-152
decline in black leadership,
    149

Blacks and Koreans, 138-140

Black Middle Class, 7-9

Black Ministers, 13-28
    Martin Luther King, Jr., 14
    NAACP, 18
    social justice, 14-18
    civil rights, 18-19
    police abuse, 22-23
    HIV/AIDS, 23-24
    personal corruption, 24
    Lyons, Henry, Dr., 25, 28

Black Panther Party, 5, 83-89
    Huey Newton, 84, 85, 88-89
    Bobby Seale, 86, 88
    Eldridge Cleaver, 87-89

Black Political Congress, 80

Black Political Parties, 78

Black Political Power, 79

Black Politicians, 73-82

Black Radical Congress, 10-11

Black Women, 61-72, 152
in prison, 61, 66-67
violence against, 63, 65
stereotypes of, 64
poverty, 65
Million Woman March, 67-70

Brown, Ron, 55-58
justice department probe, 56

C

Characteristics of,
black leadership, 147-152

Clinton, Bill, presidency, 9
Congressional Black Caucus,
40-50
affirmative action, 46-47
welfare, 47
political appointments, 49
black politicians, 73
Jesse Jackson, 96

Congressional Black Caucus,
39-50,
Republican party, 40-41, 44
Democratic party, 41, 44
racial stereotypes, 44
affirmative action, 46-47
school vouchers, 107

CORE, 2, 4-5, 62

Corporate racism, 35

Cosby, Bill, 51-55, 59

Crime,
Martin Luther King, Jr., on
violence, 36
Bill Clinton Administration,
48
Omnibus Crime Bill, 49

Cubans, 137-138

D

Decline in Black Leadership,
149

E

Economic empowerment, 36
African-American
commnity, 141-142

Education,
school vouchers, 106-108

Educational neglect, 34

Elections,
Latinos, 76-77, 82
Asians, 77, 82
blacks, 77
Democrats, 79-82
Republicans, 79- 80-82
Rainbow coalition, 81

Epsy, Mike, 73-75

H

HIV/AIDS, 23-24
black women, 66

J

Jesse Jackson, 79, 91-104

Jewish Experience, 135

K

Koreans, 138-140

L

Los Angeles, police, 13
  Margaret Mitchell, 13-14, 155-161
  Black Panther Party, 85

Louima, Abner, 110

Lyons, Henry, Dr., 25, 28

M

Malcolm X, 127-132

Martin Luther King, Jr., 14, 18-20, 26-28, 29-37
  black churches, 14-16, 20
  SCLC, 29, 32
  black family crisis, 34
  educational neglect, 34
  political apathy, 35
  corporate racism, 35
  economic empowerment, 36
  police abuse, 36
  Jesse Jackson, 96-97, 100

N

NAACP, 2, 4-5, 18, 62, 68, 115-125
  school vouchers, 105-107

Image Awards, 115-116, 118
Kweisi Mfume, 122

Nation of Islam, 2, 4-5, 10
  Million Man March, 10, 45
  Farrakhan, Louis, 10

Martin Luther King, III, 29, 31, 37-38

Myths, Anti-police, 110-113

National Affirmative Action
  Leadership Summit, 81

O

Omnibus Crime Bill, 48

P

Police abuse, 22, 36, 124, 156
  Margaret Mitchell, 13-14, 65, 155-161
  Amadou Diallo, 22, 124
  Tyisha Miller, 22, 65, 124
  Abner Louima, 110
  black community, 109-113
  Police, and the
  black community, 109

Police violence, 22

Political apathy, 35

Powell, Adam Clayton, Sr., 17-18, 26-27

Powell, Adam Clayton, Jr., 17-18, 26-27

R

Racial stereotypes, 44-45
  black women, 64

Racially, motivated violence,
  Iverson, Sherrice, 1-4

Rainbow coalition, 81, 94-95,
102

Republican party,
  school voucher, 167

Reynolds, Mel, 73

S

School Vouchers, 106-108, 113

SCLC, 2, 4-5, 29, 32, 62, 96, 105

Slavery, 136

Stereotypes, racial, 44-45, 115-
116

T

Tucker, Walter

U

Urban League, 2, 4-5, 62, 105
  school vouchers, 107

U.S. Sentencing Commission, 49

V

Vietnamese, 137

W

Welfare, 47
  black women, 66